Advance praise for
More Than I Imagined

"In this riveting and provocative memoir, John Blake transcends preconceived notions about race and the Black and White 'divide.' *More Than I Imagined* takes the reader on a compelling and courageous journey that bears witness to the realities of systemic racism, the complexity of identity within that system, and the possibilities of reconciliation. In so doing, Blake's story beautifully underscores that the personal is always political."

—Robin DiAngelo, *New York Times* bestselling author of
White Fragility

"John Blake incisively covers news of today's racial divide, but it's his own story that truly deserves to be broadcast."

—Heather McGhee, *New York Times* bestselling author of
The Sum of Us

"An incredibly moving memoir that both examines and complicates our understanding of race in America today, *More Than I Imagined* is overflowing with empathy and full of humanity. It is well worth reading."

—Clint Smith, *New York Times* bestselling author of
How the Word Is Passed

"In my role as a public thinker, many journalists reach out to me, but I tell John Blake things I don't tell any other journalist. He is sensitive to the moment and can read the racial and religious winds as they change. He has thought deeply about his own bi-racial identity and his experiences growing up in Baltimore—and he brings these keen insights to the topics he's covering. Amid the recent surge of attention given to faith and race, Blake provides the kind of steady and studied analysis that we need to understand these critical topics."

—Jemar Tisby, *New York Times* bestselling author of
The Color of Compromise

"John Blake takes us on a heartbreaking, powerful journey of personal, familial, and possibly national redemption. Truth-telling and working to confront those uncomfortable truths are at the core of this engaging and wrenching memoir."

—Carol Anderson, Ph.D., *New York Times* bestselling
author of *White Rage*

"*More Than I Imagined* impacted me far more than I could have possibly imagined. John Blake is spot-on when he writes, 'facts don't change people; relationships do.' I needed this book; our nation needs this book. Thank you, John. Highly recommend!"

—Andy Stanley, pastor, founder of North Point Ministries
and author of *Not in It to Win It*

"John Blake's memoir takes us on a twisting personal journey with a surprise around every bend. In the process, you realize he's living out the tattered history of race in America. Then comes the biggest surprise of all: This is a book of gutsy hope and not of despair, of reconciliation and not of hatred. Both sides of the racial divide need the voice that Blake is uniquely qualified to offer."

—Philip Yancey, author of *What's So Amazing About Grace?*

"*More Than I Imagined* testifies to the deepest truth that America cannot change unless Americans change. John Blake's tender, powerful reckoning with his family's history, secrets, myths, and divisions shows how we as a country can find a pathway to wholeness."

—Eric Liu, author of *Become America*

More Than I Imagined

More Than I Imagined

What a Black Man Discovered About the White Mother He Never Knew

John Blake

CONVERGENT

NEW YORK

Published in the United States by Convergent Books, an imprint of Random House, a division of Penguin Random House LLC, New York.

CONVERGENT BOOKS is a registered trademark and the Convergent colophon is a trademark of Penguin Random House LLC.

All Scripture quotations are taken from the Holy Bible, New International Version®, NIV®. Copyright © 1973, 1978 by Biblica Inc.™ Used by permission of Zondervan. All rights reserved worldwide. (zondervan.com). The "NIV" and "New International Version" are trademarks registered in the United States Patent and Trademark Office by Biblica Inc.™

LIBRARY OF CONGRESS CATALOGING-IN-PUBLICATION DATA
Names: Blake, John K., author.
Title: More than I imagined / John Blake.
Description: First edition. | New York: Convergent, 2023.
Identifiers: LCCN 2022041283 (print) | LCCN 2022041284 (ebook) |
ISBN 9780593443040 (hardback) | ISBN 9780593443057 (ebook)
Subjects: LCSH: Blake, John K., 1964- | Racially mixed people—Maryland—
Baltimore—Biography. | Racially mixed people—Georgia—Atlanta—
Biography. | Journalists—Georgia—Atlanta—Biography. | United States—
Race relations. | Baltimore (Md.)—Biography. | Atlanta (Ga.)—Biography.
Classification: LCC F190.B53 B63 2023 (print) | LCC F190.B53 (ebook) |
DDC 305.800975/26092 [B]—dc23/eng/20220830
LC record available at https://lccn.loc.gov/2022041283
LC ebook record available at https://lccn.loc.gov/2022041284

Printed in Canada on acid-free paper

convergentbooks.com

1 2 3 4 5 6 7 8 9

FIRST EDITION

Design by Ralph Fowler

Background pattern by javarman / Adobe Stock

To TL

CONTENTS

More Than I Imagined

A Painful Return Home

was about five years old when I was abducted. It was one of the most beautiful days of my childhood.

A couple of strangers lured me away from my front porch that summer afternoon. I knew they were intruders, but they somehow felt familiar. I wasn't afraid.

They were white—a young woman and an older man. I hardly ever saw white people in my Baltimore neighborhood, where most residents viewed them with suspicion, if not outright hostility. Yet they slipped past my family, took me by the hand, and led me to a baseball diamond across the street. They steered me toward the middle of a lush, sprawling field, where the woman gave me a white paper kite.

What happened next is just a fragment in my memory: squinting at the summer sky as I chased the kite, seeing the sunlight reflect off the blond hairs of the woman's pale forearms, watching as a gust of wind caught the kite and wondering if I, too, would be lifted into the air. As I peeked over my shoulder, I caught my abductors standing back to appraise me, nodding and smiling with approval. I felt wrapped in a cocoon of love.

And then it was over. I somehow ended up back at home without the strangers ever bidding me goodbye.

I never mentioned that afternoon to anyone, because I thought I would get into trouble. And a part of me hoped that someday my mysterious visitors would return.

I kept that memory tucked in my back pocket until one day, forty years later, when I was going through an old family photo album. I decided to try to solve the mystery. I called several relatives about that strange encounter. "Who was that couple?" "Why didn't anyone stop them from taking me?"

No one knew what I was talking about. Not even my younger brother, Pat, who was always at my side when we were children.

"It was a dream," Pat said, "or wishful thinking."

I was baffled. I had the kite. I had stored it in a corner of my bedroom and kept it as a memento for so long that the paper disintegrated. I had relied on the memory of that golden afternoon to help me get through the many tough days that made up my childhood.

Was Pat right? How could such a vivid memory be an invention? And how could I explain the kite that I kept as a souvenir?

On Monday, May 4, 2015, I found myself wading through a crowd of angry protesters in Baltimore, still chasing that memory. As a journalist at CNN, I'd been assigned to cover violent racial protests that had erupted in my childhood community. But another story also drew me home. It was a story about my family, about how I'd tried to move past the same kind of anger that had engulfed my neighborhood—to feel as free as I did when I was a child flying a kite on that postcard-pretty summer day.

I peeked at my cellphone. It was 4:36 P.M., and I was about to go live on national television. A sweaty, bearded CNN technician attached a microphone to the lapel of my navy-blue polo shirt. I cleared my throat as I glanced behind me at a crowd of protesters and curiosity seekers who had gathered to watch my interview. We were standing outside Baltimore's city hall complex, in a tiny park where the national media had camped out.

For more than two weeks, violent protests had rocked the city after a young Black man named Freddie Gray died in police custody. West Baltimore was filled with burning stores, smashed police cars, and at least three thousand National Guardsmen and police in riot gear facing off against angry protesters. I'd been asked to appear on air because I'd written a first-person account for CNN of what it was like to grow up in the neighborhood where Gray had lived and where the racial protests had erupted.[1]

To prepare for my television appearance, I took a quick drive to my old neighborhood to assess the damage. It was the first time I'd set foot there in about fifteen years.

I was stunned. Half the homes on the block where I grew up were vacant, boarded-up husks, some with collapsed walls spilling onto sidewalks. The sprawling baseball field where I'd flown my kite was choked with weeds and fenced off with locked gates. The constant hum of street life that I remembered—neighbors gossiping on the porches of their row houses; young men and women flirting on the corners; "Arabbers," or Black fruit vendors, calling out prices as they led their lavishly decorated horse-drawn carts down the street—was gone.

I expected looted stores and charred buildings. What I didn't know was that my community had died long before the Freddie Gray protests.

Maybe I shouldn't have been surprised. West Baltimore had one of the highest murder rates in the nation and had become a symbol of Black criminality and urban decay. It was the setting for the brutal HBO series *The Wire*. It had also become a popular conservative talking point: *Here's what happens when Black mayors run Black cities with "failed liberal policies."*[2] When some white people learn where I'm from, their eyes widen with surprise before they ask two questions: "How real was *The Wire*?" and "How did you get out?"

Poppy Harlow, the CNN anchor who was assigned to interview me, had questions of her own. Her head was bowed as she flipped through a stack of papers. She looked up and turned to me with a bright smile.

We went live. Harlow and I talked. As we approached the end of our interview, she asked me, "Just very quickly, John, I want to ask you personally, What was it like for you to come back here on assignment?"

I lowered my head and sighed. There were so many feelings to sort through.

"It was very bittersweet," I said. "It's always good to see home, but it's not good to see home like this. I feel like there are kids here who are like I was, fifteen or sixteen, and I wonder, *Can they make the journey I made?* I have doubts about that, and that's very sad."

Harlow thanked me. Our interview ended. I unclipped the microphone and stepped away, shaking my head in disappointment. The interview went so fast. There was so much more I wanted to say.

But what would I have told Harlow, knowing what I know today? I would have told her that if you think growing up as a young Black man in my neighborhood was tough, try doing it as the son of a Black father and a white mother in a place where many despise white people.

And if you want to talk about Black anger, Harlow, I have a little experience with that topic. Try reconciling with your white family while they claim they were never racist—even though they thought that Black and white people should be kept separate and even though one referred to your father as "this nigger."

Harlow invited me to appear on her show because my essay attempted to explain why so many Black men had disappeared from inner-city Baltimore. But I never told her or CNN's audience that my white mother had vanished without explanation after my birth.

That's the story I wanted to tell, but I didn't know how.

I've covered the biggest stories about race in America for the past twenty-five years, and most of those stories follow a pattern: Angry Black or brown people indict white people for their racism after something terrible happens. Chastened white people experience a "racial reckoning." The wave of moral outrage passes, the news cycle moves on, and Black and brown people continue to seethe. I get those stories. I've felt that anger.

I saw racism as an either/or proposition. Either you're a racist or you're not. There was no in-between. But my experience with the white members of my family didn't follow that script. My white relatives ended up showing me that I wasn't immune to racial prejudice and that they could teach me something about empathy and forgiveness. I never saw that story coming.

I didn't know how to tell Harlow any of that because my story doesn't fit traditional narratives about race or identity. There are elements that are too contradictory, embarrassing, and strange to share. Journalists are expected to be sober-minded operators who care only about the facts. How odd would I have sounded, telling millions of TV viewers about a series of inexplicable encounters that forced me to ask a minister one day, "Can a person seek forgiveness from beyond the grave?" How could I have explained in a sound bite that a scar over my heart, which I thought was a birthmark, turned out to be a clue to my mother's disappearance? And how could I have described why a chance street-corner encounter with two strangers—a young Black man and a white man— did more to help me overcome my anger toward my mother's family than all the books on racial reconciliation I'd ever read?

I wouldn't believe half of it if someone told me the same story. Sometimes I still have trouble believing what happened—and I was there.

My return home forced me to ask questions I'd avoided for years. Now I know why my childhood abduction meant so much to me—real or not. I've yearned most of my life to feel what I felt that day: whole, not divided, free of anger at white people for what they did to me.

I know what that type of anger does to people. I see it virtually every day in the newsroom. We're in the middle of a political and cultural civil war. Friends and family no longer talk because of politics. According to one political leader, our democracy is "in danger of imploding" because we've given up on the pursuit of a more perfect union.[3] How can we find a way forward when we live in such separate worlds?

My family was split by the same racial hatred that divides America today. We found a way to move forward and heal. If we can heal, so can others.

I'm encouraged by something the Israeli historian and philosopher Yuval Noah Harari said: "The only thing that can replace one story is another story."[4]

Mine is another story.

I used to think that if more white Americans had more information—if you showed them enough videos of unarmed Black people being harassed or killed, if you cited enough history and facts about racism—they would change. But facts don't change people; relationships do. My white family members didn't change because I shamed them with an impressive lecture on systemic racism. And facts didn't change me. There was no diversity training I could call on to help me confront my feelings of betrayal and rejection—or the white relative who terrorized me. I couldn't lift that kind of weight with intellectual muscle. I needed spiritual tools. I first had to join a community where racial reconciliation was demanded and build relationships with people I regarded as enemies. I had to experience what one scholar called "radical integration."[5]

That kind of personal journey might sound complicated. But it was driven by two simple questions I had as a boy: "Where is my mother?" and "Where do I belong?"

That story begins with a tipsy Black man wearing a panama hat, driving his beat-up Ford truck home one night. . . .

CHAPTER 1

Who Can Cling to a Ramblin' Rose?

John (age 13) with his father, Clifton, and brother, Pat

was dozing off one night when he made another of his grand entrances.

I first heard the screech of tires as his dark-blue Ford Bronco ran over a curb. Next came the mumbled curses as a set of jingling keys hit the pavement. After a long pause, the front door creaked open and heavy footsteps stumbled inside.

As I rubbed my eyes, I heard the crackling of a needle hitting a dusty record in the living room. The velvety voice of Nat King Cole filled the house, accompanied by the man's drunken rendition of Cole's "Ramblin' Rose," a country-flavored ballad about a spurned man who couldn't keep his "wild and windblown" lover, because no one can "cling to a ramblin' rose."

I sighed and flopped back on my pillow. *It's him. Dad's home for the night,* I thought.

My father, Clifton Avon Blake, Sr., was a sailor—a merchant mariner, to be exact. Our home in West Baltimore was just one of many ports of call for him. That noisy late-night entrance during my childhood was typical. Dad had a habit of popping into and out of my life at the oddest hours of the night.

He'd wait until my younger brother, Pat, and I fell asleep before tiptoeing out of the house for trips that would take him as far away as South America or Asia. The day after he left, we'd be dispatched to a foster home and an assortment of caregivers. I'd hear nothing from him for six months to a year. And then, one random night, I'd hear some commotion outside. Stumbling half-asleep to the front door, I'd catch him barging in with his stuffed green duffel bag, his panama hat, and a loopy grin on his dark-chocolate face.

He was a rambling rose. I couldn't cling to him even when he was at home. He slept like a hibernating bear for days after returning, his ragged snoring in the adjoining bedroom lulling me to sleep. And then he'd disappear to hit the neighborhood bars. The next morning, I'd find him splayed on the front porch, where he had collapsed after a night of drinking.

None of that mattered when I was a boy. He was my first hero. I could forgive him for anything. He looked like a Black Buddha, with his bald head, perpetual grin, and plump belly. He had the sculpted shoulders of a middleweight boxer and a broad, muscular chest that came from years of manual labor on ships. He thought he was hot stuff. In the summer, he paraded around our neighborhood with his shirt off, his greasy dungarees sagging so low that the crack of his ass always seemed to be visible. When I jumped onto those big shoulders to play-wrestle, he smelled like Old Spice cologne, Pall Mall cigarettes, and sweat.

"Stay cool and drink lots of water" was his credo, the cryptic phrase he invoked whenever I went to him for advice. He was the most exciting dad that a boy could ask for, a walking *National Geographic*. He had traveled to virtually every continent and had survived extended stints in three war zones and at least four brushes with death, including two in Vietnam.

He was also fun. One Saturday morning when I was about five, he summoned Pat and me to the cramped living room of our house. He was sorting through Nat King Cole records stacked on top an oak stereo console cabinet, a lit Pall Mall cigarette dangling from his lips. He wore rust-colored corduroy pants and a tight white T-shirt. An ashtray and a wad of bills stacked next to a *TV Guide* rested on the coffee table. He had just returned from a trip to Vietnam, flush with money and tales of adventure.

He looked at us with a wide smile and started humming. "I'm going to teach you the words to a song," he said. "Now watch me."

"Oh, really? Right now?" Pat said before clapping his hands in delight.

"Yup, right now. Now sit down and listen to me sing."

As we sat on the couch, he plopped a record onto the turntable.

A jaunty piano melody filled the room, and my father started shimmying to the beat as he jumped into the vocals at the precise moment Cole started to sing.

"*L is for the way you look at me,*" he sang as he smiled at us, snapping his fingers to the beat. "*O is for the only one I see. V is very, very extraordinary. E is even more than anyone that you adore can . . .*"

He then squeezed between Pat and me on the couch, draped his muscular arms around our skinny shoulders, and said, "Okay, you try."

"Nawww, Dad, play it one more time. I can't remember it," I said.

"Okay, from the top. *L is for the way you look at me . . .*"

We spent that entire morning giggling, fumbling along as we tried to remember the song. Whenever we flubbed a line, he got up from the couch and played the record from the beginning with a hearty "From the top." When we finally sang a flawless rendition, he stood up, looked down at us with a big smile, and said, "Beautiful, sons. Beautiful."

I can still sing every word to that Cole song from memory more than fifty years later.

My friends thought I had the coolest father, but I needed something more from him that he refused to give. I can't think of anyone who was more spectacularly ill-equipped to answer the two questions that preoccupied me from the beginning: "Where is my mother?" and "What is my place in the world?"

If my father was "wild and windblown," my mother was a phantom. I had no memory of her, and neither did Pat, who is less than a year younger than I am.

We shared the same mother and the same loss. We didn't know what she looked like—the color of her hair or eyes—or the sound of her voice. Nor did we have any memory of her playing with us. There was no picture of her in my father's house. I couldn't remember even once using the word *mom*.

I came into the world with half my identity amputated. My mother's name wasn't even on my birth certificate. And my dad didn't fill in those blanks. He never talked about my mother. Never explained why she was gone. Never said if she was alive or if we had relatives on her side. All he fed me were two scraps of information: Her name was Shirley, and she was white.

The white part would become a problem. Other than Pat, I didn't know anyone like me while I was growing up in inner-city Baltimore in the 1970s. When I was born in 1964, interracial marriage was illegal in nineteen states, including Maryland.[1] Three years later, the Supreme Court would declare such laws unconstitutional in *Loving v. Virginia*,[2] but interracial marriage remained taboo. Interracial couples were unheard of in my neighborhood and virtually invisible in the city. There were no visible biracial public figures like former president Barack Obama, singer Alicia Keys, or film director Jordan Peele. I never saw biracial kids in television commercials or on breakfast cereal boxes. Being "mixed" was a source of shame. We were objects of pity, "tragic mulattoes" supposedly trapped between two races, not accepted by either.

And Baltimore was no Berkeley—the city's racial climate didn't tolerate pushing racial boundaries. I'd always been told that Baltimore was part of the more racially enlightened North. But Baltimore's political leaders pioneered one of the most insidious forms of racism.

In 1910, Baltimore's City Council passed the nation's first housing segregation law,[3] which made it a crime for a Black person to move to a majority-white block. Black families in Baltimore also couldn't buy homes in many areas of the city because of redlining—a practice sanctioned by the federal housing authorities where banks refused to provide and insure home loans in or near Black communities.

I could sense those racial divisions even as a kid. There were certain neighborhoods you didn't go into if you were Black. It was a city of working-class Irish, Italian, Black, and Polish enclaves. Most city residents lived in one of the nation's largest collections of row houses: narrow, low-rise homes lined up next to one another and sharing a roofline. Many had white marble porch steps that we called "the stoop," a social center of city life where neighbors gathered to gossip, drink, and people-watch.

The skyline was as rough as the city's racial history. When I looked out my bedroom window at night, I could see a neon Domino Sugar sign illuminating the Inner Harbor, the city's port area. The rest of the skyline was dominated by a steel plant, belching smokestacks, and rusted shipping cranes and tugboats in the Inner Harbor.

My family lived in a Black community of row houses that bordered an industrial area. A Cloverland milk plant stood around the corner, and a Good Humor ice cream factory faced our narrow backyard. The aroma of sour milk and artificial chocolate hung heavy in the air.

I absorbed the city's ambient racism early on. While throwing a tantrum when I was about four, I called one of my uncles a n***** when he told me to be quiet. Not long after that, I started hearing older boys in my neighborhood tease one another with a taunt that came from a song written by a Black blues singer called Big Bill Broonzy. They'd say to one another, if you're white, you're "all right," but if you're Black, "git back."

I saw those lyrics in action one afternoon. My father was taking me on a walk through the neighborhood with Twiggy, my oldest brother. He, Stephanie, and Tony were my three older siblings from my father's marriage to a Black woman, which had ended in divorce about ten years before I was born. Twiggy was the firstborn son and carried my father's name. He was about seventeen at the time, with the same dark-chocolate complexion as my father. He had the compact build of a high school wrestler, a drooping mustache, and an Afro that made him look like a younger version of the Blaxploitation movie star Richard "Shaft" Roundtree.

As my father led me by the hand, a smiling woman approached us and looked down at me with curiosity. I was accustomed to strangers' double takes when they saw my father with me, a skinny light-skinned kid with freckles and pomade-parted hair.

"And who is this little boy?" the woman asked, bending down to look at me at eye level.

My father patted my head. "This is my son John," he said.

As the woman doted on me, my father continued to banter with her, telling her that my mother was white. But he said nothing about Twiggy, who was standing alongside us. The woman eventually stood up, tousled my hair, and walked away. She said nothing to Twiggy; neither did my father. We resumed walking, my father holding my hand as Twiggy walked slightly behind us, his face set like a stone.

I discovered that my father belonged to the "if you white, you all right" club. He treated his Blackness like an unpaid parking ticket—as something he preferred not to think about. He constantly reminded us that people thought he was Cuban or Panamanian when he was younger because he once had curly hair. He routinely introduced Pat and me to strangers by proudly announcing, "These are my little half-breed sons."

Though his first wife was Black, he boasted that she "could

pass" for white. My father was the neighborhood hell-raiser. He got into bar fights, smoked weed, mouthed off to police, and held wild parties that seemed to bring every neighborhood hustler, drug dealer, and wino into our house. But he drew the most stares from neighbors by openly bringing white prostitutes home. Sometimes it wasn't enough to bring one. He'd have two or even three by his side as he walked through the front door.

At times, he introduced us to his late-night companions. He often flipped on our bedroom light, rousing us from sleep. While we blinked, our eyes adjusting, we'd see him standing unsteadily in our bedroom doorway, his arm draped around a smiling, garishly dressed prostitute.

"I'd like you to meet my two sons," he'd say, his words slurring. "This is John, and this is Pat. . . ."

Those awkward meetings planted dark thoughts in the back of my mind. Was my mother one of those prostitutes? Did he love *her*? Or just her whiteness? But I beat back those questions. I wasn't ready to make that kind of connection as a kid. Besides, my father's silence about my mother had conditioned me to avoid questions about her or her family.

What I craved more than answers was stability: a place to belong and someone to belong to. Pat and I started staying with an aunt on the weekends when I was four, but I wanted a full-time family. So I took what my father could give me and kept my questions to myself. I accepted his silence about my mother because I discovered that there was something worse than living with such a reckless father and not knowing my mother.

It was a woman called Aunt Fannie.

·   ·   ·

The sprawling white house that stood before Pat and me looked like a haunted mansion. It was a southern-plantation-style home with a big porch flanked by large prickly bushes. The curtains were drawn tight so that no sunlight entered. A huge oak tree sat in the backyard, its gnarled branches draped like claws over the roof.

A buxom, elderly brown woman with dyed jet-black hair opened the door. The scent of stewed tomatoes and rotting vegetables made my nostrils flare.

"This is Aunt Fannie," the uncle who was dropping us off said as I looked up at the imposing woman.

My new caregiver smiled at me. It was like seeing a snake grin. She said nothing as she steered Pat and me into her house. We walked into the gloomy silence with our plastic shopping bags containing our belongings slung over our backs. When the door slammed shut behind us, I felt Pat edge closer to me for protection, bumping into my shoulder.

My father dispatched me and Patrick to foster homes because there was something he wouldn't do: give up sailing for a stateside job that would allow him to be a full-time dad. We spent up to a year at a time in foster homes while he was away. But it wasn't foster care in the traditional sense. These homes weren't licensed with the city or state. The woman we called Aunt Fannie ran an unregulated home for children in West Baltimore, no more than ten minutes from my father's house.

Pat and I eventually stayed in three such foster homes, but we stayed with Aunt Fannie the longest, about seven years, off and on. I didn't call her "Aunt" out of any sense of affection. My father ordered me to address each foster parent as "Aunt" or "Momma," but I knew they weren't related to me. There was no family warmth in any of those places. They were cold, dark, and shrouded in misery.

Aunt Fannie's was the worst. She was a "spare the rod, spoil the child" disciplinarian who relished inflicting pain. Throughout my time there, she whipped me with a tree branch, an extension cord, and a toilet plunger.

Her sadistic streak surfaced in other ways, too. She'd inform me with a cold smile on a Monday that I was going to get a whipping on Friday. Then her smile would get bigger as each day passed and my day of reckoning neared. By the time she took me to the cold, dank basement to whip me, she was virtually giggling with delight.

Her only interest in kids was monetary. She stacked Patrick and me into a bed with another boy and piled two other kids into another small bed to make more money. She never took us anywhere like a park, a baseball game, or even McDonald's. In all the years I was there, I can't remember a kind word, hug, joke, or nod of approval from her. She fed us just enough to keep us upright, forcing us to eat mushy, half-cooked food that was barely edible.

One evening, I was in the bedroom watching *Hogan's Heroes* with Pat when I heard her call, "It's time for dinner."

We headed to the kitchen, not looking forward to what she'd be putting in front of us.

She had a spacious kitchen, where she kept boxes of fruit and vegetables stacked against the wall. At times, rats from the yard would slip into the kitchen and chew into the boxes. Aunt Fannie placed wooden traps throughout the kitchen to catch them. At night, I'd hear the traps snap shut. She often didn't bother to empty them, so when we schlepped into the kitchen that evening, I could see the broken carcasses of two rats resting against the wall. I looked away, stifling the nausea welling up in my throat.

She placed a bowl of stewed tomatoes before each of us—a dish she loved to serve and we hated to eat. But we were too afraid to say anything. I took a breath and started swallowing, looking out the window, thinking of playing baseball to keep my mind off the horrible taste and the dead rats.

Pat, just seven years old, dropped his spoon against the bowl. He looked up at Aunt Fannie, who was setting glasses on the table. "Aunt Fannie, I don't like this," he mumbled.

She placed her hands on her hips and glared at Pat. "You better eat that, boy."

Pat sighed, picked up his spoon, and started easing the tomatoes into his mouth, grimacing with each gulp.

I nodded at him, encouraging him to keep on.

Pat dropped the spoon again. He turned away from the table, lowered his head, and vomited on the floor.

I froze in my chair, not knowing what to do. I looked at Aunt Fannie, who showed no reaction. She looked at the floor and then looked at Pat. "You're going to clean that plate," she said.

I started to reach out to Pat but placed my hands under my lap, too scared to move. Pat slowly resumed eating the tomatoes in silence as I watched. Aunt Fannie turned her back to us and started washing dishes. After Pat finished, she made him clean up the vomit. I quickly and quietly helped him. As we walked out of the kitchen, I turned to Pat and rested my hand on his shoulder. He finally teared up when we headed to the bedroom.

There were worse moments than that night at Aunt Fannie's. Two memories linger.

One night when I was about four, the first year Pat and I were at Aunt Fannie's, I went to the bathroom after everyone fell asleep. I clicked on the light, closed the door, and stood in the cramped space to relieve myself. As I flushed and turned away from the toilet, I realized that my mouth felt so dry. I tried to reach the faucet on the bathroom sink to turn on the water, but I was too short.

I swallowed again. My throat felt like sandpaper.

Thirst and hunger were common sensations at Aunt Fannie's. She wouldn't allow us to enter the kitchen except to eat the wretched meals she threw together. I was too afraid to ask her for food or water at any other time of the day, so I often felt weak and thirsty.

On this night, I looked down at the clear water in the toilet, and a wild thought entered my mind: I could drink that water. I bent down and drank from the commode. The water was colder than I'd expected.

From that night on, after I knew Aunt Fannie was asleep, I'd go into the bathroom to drink from the toilet. Only later would I learn that Patrick went through the same ritual to satisfy his thirst. It was the only way we could get cold water without risking her anger.

Aunt Fannie's also functioned as an ad hoc daycare. At the end of the workday, the doorbell rang, and the sounds of children scurrying through the hallway, squealing with delight, filled the house. Their parents had come to take them home for the night. The only other kid that stayed full-time with Aunt Fannie was Jimmy, another biracial kid whose parents had abandoned him. Neither I nor Pat ever talked to Jimmy about the bond we shared. He was a bully I often had to fight to keep him away from Pat.

I stayed in my bedroom most of the time, but one day when I was about seven, I decided to watch this ritual. When the front door opened, I saw a woman scoop her smiling daughter into her arms while the girl yelled, "Mommy!"

When they left, I walked into the living room, parted a curtain, and watched them drive away. Even after their car disappeared, I kept looking down the empty street for someone else to arrive. That someone was my father. I kept looking, hoping that my love for him would somehow cross oceans and continents and summon him home. I'd see him materialize on the horizon, coming toward me with a big smile, his bouncy walk, and that dirty green duffel bag slung over his shoulder. This time, I'd be the one who would jump into his arms as he picked me up to take me home.

But no one appeared. I turned around and melted back into the gloomy silence of the foster home. I felt utterly alone.

I never complained to my father or his relatives. Nor did Patrick. Besides, we didn't know any other kind of life; this was all we had. Every weekend, we stayed with an actual aunt, my father's sister. But I never revealed to her how I felt. I was afraid Aunt Fannie would somehow find out and take it out on me or Patrick.

"You were like a little robot," Twiggy said years later. "You just did what you were told and didn't complain. Nobody knew anything was wrong."

But I knew. I counted the days until my childhood was over. I developed a ritual with calendars. I studied them with longing. When Aunt Fannie wasn't looking, I'd pull out a massive calendar from a box in the kitchen and flip the pages until I got to the year when I'd be old enough to leave her house. I'd note the date on that calendar and tell myself that if I could just hold out until then, I'd be all right.

One day when I was about eight, I couldn't wait anymore. I decided to act.

It was summertime, one of those glorious days in West Baltimore when everybody seemed to be out on the streets: kids riding bicycles, neighbors talking on the stoop. The song "Joy to the World" by Three Dog Night blasted from someone's radio and a group of boys played stickball in a nearby alley. I put on my favorite outfit—a navy-blue-and-white baseball cap, a purple cotton shirt, orange athletic wristbands, and pin-striped cutoff jeans—and took a deep breath.

Somebody's gotta be there. Somebody's gotta be there, I kept telling myself, trying to pump myself up for what I'd find at my house.

I waited until Aunt Fannie left the living room to watch one of her soap operas in her bedroom. Then I tiptoed out the front door, glancing behind me to make sure she wasn't there. I shut the door, skipped down the front steps, and hit the pavement. I turned to my right and squinted through the haze of exhaust fumes toward a baseball field in the distance. That field was next to my father's house.

Somebody's gotta be there, I told myself again. *Somebody.*

My father was overseas, but I thought if I could make it to his house, another relative would be there to take me in. *I'll tell them all about how mean Aunt Fannie is, and then they'll take me back to get Patrick.*

I started to walk to the baseball field, then broke into a light jog. I arrived at an intersection and stood on the corner. Cars whizzed by, car horns blared, and mass-transit-bus engines revved as they picked up passengers. I looked to my right and saw a liquor store. People walked by, some shooting curious glances at me. I stepped off the street corner.

That's when it hit me: Even if I made it to my father's house, chances were no one would be there. He was halfway around the world, and the house was probably empty. I'd have to return to Aunt Fannie's and explain my absence, and then I'd get a whipping. I looked longingly again at the baseball field, its lush green grass shimmering in the distance like an oasis.

My shoulders slumped in defeat. I turned and walked back to Aunt Fannie's. I slipped into the house without her knowing I had left.

Whenever my father returned home, he seemed oblivious to our torment. He never asked me or Patrick about the foster homes. He never stopped at the foster homes to pick us up when he returned from the ships. He never asked me anything about Aunt Fannie. And I was too afraid to tell.

My father wasn't a religious man, but he saw God's handiwork in our stay at Aunt Fannie's. "I couldn't ask for no better," he once said of those foster homes. "I thanked God every day for looking out for us. God really stepped in. Everything just fell in place."

It did for him, but not for us.

The open sea offered him more possibilities for fun and freedom than watching his two sons ever could. While living in Baltimore during the Jim Crow era, he had to endure daily indignities. There were places he couldn't go and things he couldn't say.

One day while driving a mass-transit bus in the 1950s for part-time work, my father was punched in the face by a white man because he was so enraged that the city had decided to hire Black drivers. At sea, my father steered tankers through the Panama and Suez canals, chatting about music and shared adventures with white men at his side. At home, police stopped him on the streets when they saw him cavorting with white women. At sea, he could be with any woman he wanted. He was an American man whose pockets were stuffed with dollars, hitting foreign shores at the peak of America's global power in the post–World War II era.

He didn't talk about racism much, but once he told me with a bitter chuckle, "I've been called nigger so much that I thought it was my middle name: Clifton Nigger Blake."

I asked him one time if he ever got lonely on the ship, hoping he would say he missed me or Patrick.

"I never got lonely because there were a lot of young guys on the ship," he cheerfully told me. "We always had a lot of fun. It was an adventure. It was fun to be out there."

Meanwhile, I was marooned in those foster homes. I had to find a way to save myself and Patrick; no one was coming to rescue us.

So I became a scavenger. Like a young Robinson Crusoe, I pieced together any scraps of hope I could find to help me forget where I was, even if that escape was only in my mind.

One of them came through a man Aunt Fannie instructed us to call Mr. Bill.

He seemed to materialize one day at Aunt Fannie's house. He was an elderly Black man who stayed in a spare room next to the kitchen. I didn't know if he was a relative, a boyfriend, a lover— that was all beyond my boyhood comprehension.

He was small and wiry, with a pencil mustache, a crew cut, and a handsome, craggy face with high cheekbones. He was always neatly dressed as if he were going to church.

When we'd cross Mr. Bill's path in those gloomy, labyrinthine staircases at Aunt Fannie's, his face would light up with a smile and he'd say, "Helloooooo, Pat Pat and John John."

"Hello, Mr. Bill," we'd respond in unison, smiling at our new housemate.

I was about to go to sleep one night at Aunt Fannie's when I heard something other than the snap of rat traps coming from the kitchen. It was a deep humming sound, like an idling engine.

"Hey, Pat, you hear that?" I asked, turning to Pat, but he was sound asleep. So was Jimmy. I eased the covers off the bed and tiptoed to the kitchen. The sound grew louder. Curious, I padded to the kitchen doorway, hid behind the door, and peeked inside. There was Mr. Bill sitting alone at the kitchen table, with a black leather Bible and a hymnbook. He took off his silver glasses, rubbed his eyes, and put the glasses back on. Then he sighed, opened the hymnal, and started to sing in a rumbling Barry White baritone:

> *All to Jesus I surrender;*
> *Humbly at his feet I bow,*
> *Worldly pleasures all forsaken;*
> *Take me, Jesus, take me now.*
> *I surrender all,*
> *I surrender all. . . .*

A serene, faraway look came over his face. He closed his eyes and smiled.

What is he talking about? I thought. *Did he steal something? Why does he have to surrender?*

I sat on the cold wooden floor in the hallway and continued to listen to Mr. Bill's soothing voice. Finally, when I started to get sleepy, I peeked inside again to make sure he hadn't seen me. Then I darted to my bedroom, sneaked into the bed, and threw the covers over myself. Pat rustled next to me. I fell asleep to the sound of Mr. Bill's voice still rumbling from the kitchen.

"Mr. Bill unplugged" became my evening entertainment. I'd return to my kitchen hideout whenever I'd hear him start to sing. "I Surrender All" was the only song I ever heard from him.

He pretended not to notice me. And his decision to allow me to stay there night after night meant so much to me. It was the only adult warmth I ever experienced in those foster homes. With that small act, Mr. Bill showed me that kindness could exist in even the coldest places.

I had another reason not to give in to despair: Patrick. I was my younger brother's keeper. I couldn't wallow in sadness or self-pity; it would demoralize Pat.

Pat was small for his age, so skinny that his nickname was "Bones." He walked around with his shoulders perpetually slumped, eyes downcast. He was so quiet that a classmate stopped him at school one day and asked, "Can you talk?" When something bad would happen in the foster home, I'd look up to see him looking at me for reassurance. He never seemed as bothered by what was happening to us as I was. "I wasn't worried about anything as long as you were within six feet of me," he told me years later.

Once when I was about seven, Patrick and I were walking through an alley near Aunt Fannie's when we were surrounded by four older boys. This was the 1970s. The faces of missing kids weren't plastered on milk cartons. Even strict adults like Aunt Fannie allowed their children to play and roam outside.

The leader of the boys picked up a jagged rock and advanced toward us while his buddies closed in.

I looked at Pat and pushed him behind me.

"Run!" I told him.

Pat looked at me in confusion.

"Run!" I said again before he scurried away.

I scampered up a mound of debris piled in the alley to give myself some high ground; then I turned and faced the boys. I balled my small fists and looked at the leader again. *If anything happens, go for him first,* I said to myself.

Suddenly the oddest feeling came over me. I was no longer

afraid or nervous. A wave of peace settled over me. Everything seemed to move in slow motion. I faced the boys, saying nothing, with my legs spread and fists held high. The leader looked at me, hesitated, and then looked at the others, who stared back at him. I heard the click of rocks hitting the ground. Without saying a word, the group turned and walked away.

I quickly returned to Pat and picked up with our play as if nothing had happened.

Something else gave me strength, something I could hold in the palm of my hand: a library card. There was no internet back then, no video games. There were just three channels on the small black-and-white TV set at Aunt Fannie's, and we were allowed to watch for only small windows of time.

A book was the one form of escape I could control. Even Aunt Fannie left me alone when she saw me reading. I lost myself in stories about heroes: Daniel Boone, Davy Crockett, and Audie Murphy, the most decorated American soldier in World War II. When I went to bed at night, I constructed elaborate stories to spin an alternate reality. Like an undersized Walter Mitty, I inserted myself into heroic tales, where I found myself fighting off Indians with Crockett at my side or storming a Nazi bunker on D-Day with Murphy cheering me on. On other occasions, I relived that memory of flying a white kite with my friendly abductors. It was the only way I could go to sleep.

Aunt Fannie kept a huge beige Bible on her living room table. I never saw her read it, but I dipped into it when she wasn't around and read stories about brave young men like David, who slew Goliath, and Joseph, the boy with "the coat of many colors" who became the second-most-powerful man in Egypt despite being sold into slavery by his family.

I was also fascinated by the mythological Greek hero Theseus.

He was the warrior who entered the labyrinth to kill the dreaded half-man, half-bull Minotaur. Then after slaying the monster, he used a ball of string to find his way out of the maze.

I didn't realize it at the time, but these stories were the string I used to guide myself through my own labyrinth. Reading them was like putting on psychological armor. I subconsciously extracted lessons from them to strengthen myself for my trials. I also found in them other models for manhood. My father never wrote or called while he was away. But when I opened a book, these heroes became my surrogate fathers, my teachers.

I was also able to escape through a story of my own, an inadvertent gift from my father.

He didn't like talking about my time as a toddler. Wouldn't answer questions about my mom. He wouldn't even answer a question I had about the jagged, dime-sized scar above my heart. It had always been there, but I couldn't figure out how I'd gotten it. Was it a birthmark or some injury? Whenever I pressed for more information, he would change the subject.

But there was one story about my birth that he loved to tell.

I wasn't supposed to live, he'd say. My mother had a troubled pregnancy. I was born prematurely, weighing two or three pounds. The doctor put me in an incubator because I had problems breathing. My father said he went home the day I was born not expecting to see me alive again.

He got a call from the doctor later that day.

"He told me I might want to see you before you leave the world," he said. "And then in the next half hour, he called back and said, 'You don't need to come in. We took the oxygen off, and he's breathing on his own.' I never forgot that."

Still, stories can't replace the presence of an actual father. As the years went on, the pain of seeing him depart was becoming unbearable. His homecomings began feeling almost cruel. They meant that we could escape the foster home for longer than a weekend. But then my father would leave again, and we'd return to Aunt Fannie's.

As I approached the age of ten, I became more vocal. I begged him not to return to sea. I asked if I could join the merchant marine and sail away with him, but he just laughed. I even plotted to become a stowaway on one of his journeys.

It was around that time in the spring that I decided I was going to make him stay. I could see the signs of his impending departure, and I started to panic. The wad of cash he carried was just about gone. The women and the winos weren't coming around the house anymore. He slowly started clearing out his bedroom, packing his duffel bag when I wasn't looking. He could tell by then how much it hurt me and Patrick when he left us for the ship.

I got out of bed that night, padded down the hallway, and jumped into bed with him while he was sleeping. I shook his muscular arm.

"Dad. Dad. You're not going on the ship tonight, are you?"

"No, go to sleep," he said groggily before turning away from me.

"Dad, won't you stay this time?"

He began snoring.

I trotted back to bed and made a pact with myself. I would stay awake all night, and at the first stirring of activity in my father's bedroom, I would run down the hallway to block his departure. He wouldn't escape this time.

I sat up in bed like a soldier on sentry duty, listening for any suspicious sound. But I couldn't stay awake, and I eventually dozed off. I woke up the next morning and panicked. I ran down the narrow hallway to my father's bedroom and swung open the door.

I slumped to the ground. The room was empty. The duffel bag, the panama hat, and the bars of Lava soap he stocked up on were all gone. I could still smell him: his Old Spice cologne and his Pall Mall cigarettes. But by that point, he was already headed to some distant port. Who knew when I would see him next?

I lowered my head and walked down the hallway to wake my younger brother. We knew the routine. A relative would be downstairs, waiting to take us to Aunt Fannie's.

I lived in a constant state of waiting. Waiting for the weekend when I would stay with a relative. Waiting until I would be old enough to leave Aunt Fannie's. And waiting for the only sounds that allowed me to sleep well: my father bursting through the front door and singing along with Nat King Cole deep into the night.

CHAPTER 2

Black Boy, White Boy

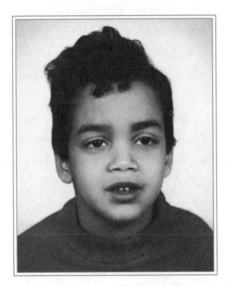

John in second grade

would never share this story if there hadn't been a witness. It was beyond strange or frightening. It was inexplicable. It took place in my father's house one summer night when I was about ten while he was away at sea. Something awakened me from a deep sleep. As soon as my eyes flew open, I gasped. My heart was racing. My body was telling me I was in danger, though my mind hadn't figured out why. I lay trembling in the darkness, afraid to survey my bedroom for fear of what I might find.

It wasn't hot that night, but I was covered in a cold sweat. I was on the top of a bunk bed with Pat below me. I was lying on my side in a fetal position, knees drawn to my chest, my arms and legs paralyzed. I shifted my eyes to the corner of our bedroom. That's when I saw him.

A thin white man stood with his back to me, rummaging through my dresser. He moved with an unearthly lightness, floating above the floor—yes, *floating*. His torso was visible, but there were no legs below his waist. He paid me no mind while he pulled drawers out of my dresser as if he were searching for something.

This can't be real! I told myself. *This must be a dream.*

I blinked to make sure I wasn't dreaming. I looked again. He was still there. My heart started to thump, like it was going to beat a hole through my chest. *I have to tell Pat,* I thought.

When I tried to yell out, no sound came from my mouth. All I could manage was to stare at the man as I lay on my left side, sweat stinging my eyes.

The man was short and wiry, with high cheekbones and a thick coal-black crew cut. Slanting light from the ice cream factory streamed through the window, illuminating his torso. He was wearing a banana-yellow, short-sleeved shirt that looked like vintage clothing from the 1950s. I could make out only the back of his head and his profile. I'd never seen him before. I waited for him to turn and pounce on me, but he kept his back to me.

I looked at him for what seemed like hours, panting and sweating before finally drifting off to sleep.

When I awakened the next morning, I jumped out of bed and

took a step toward my dresser. I stopped when I saw something on the green linoleum bedroom flooring. There was a trail of blood-red boot prints leading to my dresser, some edging up to the foot of my bed, facing me. I followed the trail into the hallway, down the stairs, and out to the front porch. The footprints were faint but clear. I ran back to the bedroom, hurtling up the steps two at a time, and saw Pat. He was standing at the foot of our bed, staring at the same footprints.

"Did you see something last night?" I asked him.

"Yeah, I did."

"Was it a man?"

"Yup."

"What did he look like?"

Patrick described the same man. We stared at each other in silence, trying to figure out the identity of our visitor. I walked to my dresser and pulled open one of the drawers the man had been poking through. Something was missing. He had taken something that belonged to me.

It had to have been the most vivid nightmare I'd ever experienced. But I couldn't figure out how Pat had seen the same apparition. Maybe we conjured a white visitor to compensate for the absence of our white family. Or maybe, I thought at the time, someone had played an elaborate prank on us. I had no frame of reference for this kind of experience. I tried to pretend it had never happened. So did Pat. We didn't talk about our nocturnal visitor again until we were adults. Besides, who would believe us? We had enough problems to deal with.

The timing of the visit, though, was somehow fitting. I was

already starting to associate white men with fear. I didn't need to see a white apparition to be leery of them. I got that message from living in West Baltimore.

The neighborhood where I grew up in the 1970s was more than thirty years away from the violent protests that followed Freddie Gray's death. But the seeds of fear and anger were being planted in my neighborhood, and in me.

I was playing catch with Pat in the backyard of Aunt Fannie's not long after our dreadful nocturnal encounter when I heard footsteps thundering toward us from a yard next door. I turned and saw a heavy twenty-something Black woman crash into Aunt Fannie's chain-link fence, lumber over it, and stagger forward.

"Who is that? What is she . . ." I said, my arm poised above my head in a throwing motion.

The woman was cradling a shopping bag bulging with clothes, their price tags still attached. She took off running through Aunt Fannie's yard without glancing toward us. Sweat beaded on her forehead.

More huffing and puffing came from the same direction. I turned and saw a muscular, middle-aged white police officer climb over the same fence, break into a clumsy sprint, and catch the woman, taking her down with a lunging tackle. He scrambled on top of her, pinned her arms with his knees, and hit her in the face with a series of clipped, savage blows.

"Get off me!" the woman yelled as tears rolled down her face.

The officer kept punching her, his face turning red. "Stay down! Stay down!" he shouted.

I stepped back, grabbed Pat, and steered him behind me.

The woman was a shoplifter, the clothes from her bag spilling out into the yard. The officer hauled her to a standing position, cuffed her while she cried hysterically, and dragged her away. He didn't say anything to Pat or me or even look in our direction, even though his beating of that woman had taken place no more than ten yards from us.

My eyes narrowed in anger as I watched him. I wanted to reach out, push the officer away, take the cuffs off that woman, and tell her to run. But I couldn't move—I was afraid of what the officer would do to me.

I plopped the ball into my glove.

"Let's do something else," I said to Pat.

He said nothing as we walked back into Aunt Fannie's with our heads bowed.

I looked over my shoulder at the skid marks in the dirt where the white police officer had dragged the Black woman away.

I didn't get the name of the officer that day, but later I learned that some called him "the man." Others preferred "honky" or "cracker."

Those were just some of the racist epithets I overheard Black people use to describe white people. No one ever sat me down and said white people were bad. Yet I absorbed that message because of what I saw and heard. Hatred of white people was like humidity in my world—I couldn't help but breathe it in. Much of the anger at white people centered on white police officers. We routinely saw them beat and humiliate Black people.

One of my biggest fears was that a white police officer would attack my father and carry him away. One day when I was about ten, it almost happened. My father wouldn't pay a cabbie's fare that he deemed too high, so the cabbie called the police. I watched and cried like a baby as the white officers handcuffed my father. I feared they would beat him. So I quickly reached into his pocket, grabbed a wad of bills and coins, and threw the money at the officers.

The angry look on my father's face evaporated, and he agreed to pay the fare. One of the officers unlocked his handcuffs. My father walked toward me with a tender smile, rubbed my hair, and drew me into a hug while I continued to sniffle.

Everybody seemed to have a story about racist white people. I overheard my Black relatives complaining about dealing with racist bosses, who were identified by the universal designation "Mr. Charlie." I eavesdropped in Black barbershops, hearing Black men talk about "crackers." I heard a Black pastor say during a Sunday morning sermon, "You know you can't trust no white folks." The Black congregation answered with nodding heads and a chorus of amens.

Yet most of my hostility toward white people was shaped by what I didn't see: ordinary white people living among us in West Baltimore. It's easier to despise a group of people you have no personal contact with.

I was growing up in the Jim Crow North: segregated much like the South, minus the White Only signs. Many white people in Baltimore were just as opposed to living next door to Blacks as their counterparts in places like Mississippi.

When the Supreme Court ruled in the landmark 1954 *Brown v. Board of Education* decision that the "separate but equal" doctrine that was used to justify racially segregated schools was unconstitutional, it sparked "white flight" across America. White families in places like Baltimore moved to the suburbs to avoid sharing neighborhoods and public schools with Black families. That exodus accelerated with the racial unrest that spread through American cities in the 1960s.

Long before abandoned, boarded-up row houses became a symbol of Baltimore's urban decay, the city was bleeding white residents. White people were fleeing Baltimore as early as the mid-nineteenth century as more Black people moved into the city before the Civil War.[1] The city's population peaked at 950,000 in 1950 but fell below 600,000 by 2020.[2] Fewer people meant less money from property taxes and other fees. And less money meant fewer resources to address needs like abandoned houses, failing public schools, and trash collecting in the streets.

Sometimes white flight wasn't gradual; it seemed instantaneous. I heard a childhood friend tell Twiggy what happened after his family became the first Black family to move into an all-white neighborhood in West Baltimore during the late 1950s.

"When I went to school in the morning, the neighborhood was all white," he told Twiggy with a sardonic laugh. "When I came home later that day, it was all Black."

Seeing a white person in my neighborhood was like seeing Bigfoot. People stopped and gawked.

That racial isolation extended to school. During my entire time in Baltimore's public schools—from Head Start to high school graduation—I saw only one white student. She was a stout blond girl with red cheeks who walked silently through my junior high hallways with her head down. Everybody stopped talking and stared when she walked by. No one said anything to her. I felt sorry for her, but I wouldn't dare greet her in the hallway because I didn't want to be ostracized for reaching out. We all gave her the silent treatment.

I thought the racial makeup of my school was normal—white people just didn't go to school with us. But the racial makeup of my school wasn't accidental. It was deliberate. The federal government tried to force Baltimore's public schools to integrate. But city politicians and school board members successfully fought school integration orders in federal courts.[3]

The only white people I had any ongoing contact with were

authority figures: teachers, police officers, or bill collectors who stopped by the house looking for my father. I never met a white kid my age.

White people were a spectral presence in my life long before I ever saw the apparition of the old white man. I saw them as a vast, homogenous group devoid of any individuality. They were the people I saw on TV who had everything—grand homes, manicured lawns, and the fanciest cars—while I had to drink toilet water in a foster home.

I didn't know how hostile I was toward white people until I stumbled onto an article in a newspaper lying on my father's coffee table when I was in high school. The headline blared, "Black Man Is Killed by Mob in Brooklyn: Attack Called Racial."

The article recounted how a Black man was assaulted with two companions after their car stalled in a white section of Brooklyn one night. They were attacked by a mob of about twenty bottle-throwing white youths yelling, "Nigger, get out of here!" The mob pulled the thirty-four-year-old Black transit worker from the car and murdered him "in a blur of fists and feet," the article read.[4]

I tossed the paper back onto the table and stood up. My temples started to throb. *That could have been me,* I thought. I had become stranded in a white neighborhood about five years earlier with Pat and a buddy. As we walked home, a carload of white men drove by and yelled, "Niggers!" I was afraid they were going to stop and attack us.

I then recalled the white police officer pummeling the Black woman in front of Pat and me at Aunt Fannie's.

I needed some fresh air. I walked outside and stood on the front porch. I scanned the sidewalk and saw many of the Black guys I knew in my neighborhood: tough, wiry young men in tank tops and cutoff jean shorts hanging out on the corner, shadow-boxing and laughing.

"I wish some of them crackers would come around here and try some of that shit," I muttered as I thought about the mob.

Another thought occurred to me. What would *I* do if I saw a white person walking through our neighborhood? Would I join my friends, who would no doubt make any young white man pay for prancing through our neighborhood?

My answer was immediate: I'd have to hurt them too. I had to show them that *they* had no business in *our* neighborhood. I turned and walked back into the house, more disturbed by what I had read than by my thoughts.

This brewing anger, though, presented a peculiar challenge for me: My mom was one of those white people. How could I hate white people when my own mother was white?

My solution: I became a closeted biracial person. I pretended the white side of my identity didn't exist. I wouldn't tell anyone that my mother was white. I was too ashamed. It was a secret that I kept from even my closest friends. I pretended that my mother was Black and marked it as such on school forms. I even stopped including my middle name—Kennedy—in my signature. I was named after the nation's first Irish Catholic president, in honor of my mother's Irish heritage, but I wanted no reminder of that side of me.

I had to look the part to play the part as well. No more pomade-parted hair, which my father preferred. I grew a curly Afro by the time I was a teenager and purchased an Afro pick with a handle styled in a Black Power salute. I got an assist from Twiggy, who persuaded my father to stop slathering Pat's and my hair with pomade before we went to church in our overcoats and suits and ties.

Twiggy was relieved when we ditched our pomade for Afro Sheen hairspray.

"That shit be shining in the sun," Twiggy said, referring to our slickened hair. "Y'all looked like gangsters. I told Dad, 'They don't need it. Let 'em go natural.'"

Then, over dinner one night, I broke the news to my father: "Stop introducing me as 'mixed' or 'half-breed.' I'm Black."

He frowned. "You're not Black," he said, raising his voice and dropping his fork onto his plate. "When you say you're Black, you deny your mother."

I didn't respond, because I didn't want to argue. Inside, I fumed. How could I deny someone I didn't know?

Denying my whiteness, though, wasn't hard most of the time. I was able to "pass" as all Black because most Black people are racially mixed in some way or another. That's part of the legacy of rape during slavery. We're accustomed to seeing a variety of skin hues, facial features, and hair textures in our midst. Still, I couldn't escape some classmates' suspicions—just being light was bad enough. My stomach tightened when a kid in school or on the street called me "white boy," "honky," or "cracker." Those were fighting words.

Kids fought all the time in my neighborhood. But my fights took on a racial dimension. When the fists started flying, my anger only deepened as other kids gathered around me and the invariably darker kid I was fighting to chant, "It's a fight! It's a fight! Between a nigger and a white!"

Pat got it worse because he was even lighter. One day he was walking home alone from junior high school along a deserted stretch of railroad tracks when he heard a chorus of voices behind him.

"Hey, white boy! Hey, you. Come here!"

He didn't look up. He thought they were talking to someone else. Then something started to pepper the ground around him. The boys were throwing rocks at him—not small ones, but the big, jagged rocks that line railway beds.

He turned to look. One hit him just above his right eye. Warm blood trickled down his face. He started running and kept running as they pursued him. He finally outran the boys and arrived home, trembling and bleeding.

He was more hurt by being called white than by being hit with stones. "This is stupid! So stupid!" he told me.

Pat and I wanted the same thing: a place to belong. Despite how poorly we were treated, Black people were all we knew. West Baltimore was our home. Our neighborhood felt like an extended family, despite the taunts we endured.

This connection was fostered by my community's geography. It was virtually impossible to socially distance from your neighbors in West Baltimore. Everybody on my block lived on top of or next to one another. I heard couples arguing, having sex, throwing parties. Everybody knew everybody's business.

This connection was also a by-product of the time we were in. Being Black was about as cool as you could get in the 1970s, when I came of age. Black was beautiful: People wore huge Afros, platform shoes, and tight jeans. We all tuned in to *Soul Train*, "the hippest trip in America," to steal the latest dance moves or listen to hits by Marvin Gaye or Earth, Wind & Fire. Young men strutted down the block with flamboyant, pimp-style walks and gave "dap"—elaborate handshakes featuring bumping fists and hooking fingers—to each other.

The constant energy in the streets deepened the feeling of community. Something was always happening: people hanging in front of the corner store, exchanging lottery tips; men sitting on the stoop, flirting with shapely women passing by ("Girl, that can't be jelly, because jam don't shake like that!"); elderly ladies with their arms folded over ample bosoms, watching children play on the sidewalk. This was a pre-internet era when kids hardly ever stayed inside.

Most of the people in my community were so close that we usually didn't address one another with the "government-issue" names like white people used. I knew several "Peanuts," a "Pookie," a "Boonie," a "Peaches," and a "Bucket-Head." I even had close relatives whose real names I never learned. I had a first cousin we called "Puddin'" and another cousin called "Chunky." I would have been stumped if you'd asked me their first names.

What bonded us more than anything else was a sense of shared vulnerability. We all knew what it was to suffer from the whims and cruelty of white people. I felt an instant bond whenever I saw a Black person in public, no matter how far I ventured.

Twiggy picked up Pat and me to take us to his new condo in rural Pennsylvania one weekend. He was the first person in our family to graduate from college. He had just graduated from Hampton Institute with a business degree, gotten a job with John Deere selling farming equipment, and purchased a sky-blue Pontiac Firebird. As we drove through a small town, Twiggy came to a stoplight. He glanced to his right, where another young Black man sat in his idling car. They locked eyes and gave each other "the nod"—that almost imperceptible lowering of the head that Blacks use to signal racial solidarity.

"Do you know him?" I asked Twiggy, confused.

"Don't have to," Twiggy told me as the light turned green and he eased his sports car forward. "He's a brother."

Since my father was overseas so much, Twiggy, who was fourteen years older than I was, became a father figure to Patrick and me. He taught us how to use cologne ("Don't bathe in it; just a little touch will do"), gave me "the birds and the bees" talk (I burst out laughing in the middle of it), and told me what the ladies liked ("Always have your shoes shined; that's the first thing they look at").

He was the coolest Black man I knew. He had grown up to be a smooth, trim young man with a neat Afro, a megawatt smile, and a confident bearing. He always seemed to have three things with him whenever I saw him: a leather jacket, a packet of Dentyne gum, and a pretty woman. He bought a winter coat for Pat when my brother outgrew his clothes. And he took us shopping with him when he purchased his first business suits and car.

But because he was a young man trying to establish his own life, there was one thing he wasn't prepared to do—take us from the foster home. By the time I was twelve, we were still spending our weekdays in Aunt Fannie's "gulag." It had become unbearable. I had to do something.

One day, I finally did.

On a Friday afternoon at Aunt Fannie's, I went into the bedroom I shared with Patrick and announced, "We're going home."

Pat's eyes widened. He said nothing, immediately walked over to the dresser, and pulled out his clothes to stuff into a plastic shopping bag.

My hands shook. I reprised an affirmation I had once used years ago in a similar situation: *Somebody's gotta be there,* I told myself. *Somebody's gotta be there.*

For years I had dreamed of running away while staring at so many calendars. Now it was time to act.

I waited until Aunt Fannie left on an errand. Then I dumped

my clothes into a plastic shopping bag. Patrick and I tiptoed through the house and gently closed the front door behind us.

I slung my bag over my shoulder, leading the way, and Pat and I started walking in silence toward my father's house. My heart hammered in my chest, but I didn't look back. I was afraid I might see Aunt Fannie coming after us.

After we crossed the first major intersection, I picked up the pace while Pat stumbled to keep up.

We entered one of my favorite sections of West Baltimore, a bucolic road called Gwynns Falls Parkway. It's a historic landmark, a two-mile stretch that features a wide median shadowed by huge maple and elm trees. It looks like a road winding through an enchanted forest.

As we entered the parkway, putting distance between ourselves and that hated foster home, my heart rate started to slow. It was a radiant summer day. I looked up at the trees. The sunlight beamed through the leaves and hit our faces. I turned to Patrick, and we exchanged loopy grins. We then turned and looked at the road ahead.

Without saying anything, we started to skip and run. The journey was only 1.4 miles, but it felt like an epic trek.

I saw a familiar landmark in the distance—the baseball field right next to my father's house. We hit the block where my father lived and took a deep breath when we walked onto the porch. The front door was closed, and all the front windows were shut. We knew our father was overseas.

Somebody's gotta be there, I repeated to myself. *Somebody's gotta be there.*

I knocked on the door. No answer. I knocked again. My shoulders slumped, and I glanced at Pat, grimacing. Suddenly I heard something stir behind the front door. A lock unfastened. Then the door swung open. Twiggy stood there.

"What are you guys doing here?" he asked.

He looked over our shoulders to see if any adults had driven us there. He was wearing a wrinkled Hampton Institute T-shirt and had a bemused look on his face. We must have awakened him from a nap.

"We're staying," I said. I walked past him before he could argue and threw my bag of clothes on the living room couch. "We're not going back."

Twiggy said nothing; he just looked at me. I stood my ground, with Pat behind me. The baffled expression on my older brother's face softened.

"Okay, if you stay, these are the rules. . . ." he said.

I may have seemed resolute in running away, but it was a calculated gamble. I'd heard that Twiggy was going to move into my father's house that summer to save money on rent before starting a new job. I figured if we showed up on his doorstep, he wouldn't turn us away. And if Aunt Fannie came looking, he would defend us.

I wouldn't remember that I had run from Aunt Fannie's until more than forty years later when Pat and Twiggy reminded me. I'd blocked it out because I'd been so afraid at the time.

Our arrival brought us immediate relief, but it altered Twiggy's summer plans. He'd planned on having fun while Dad was away.

He scolded us in mock indignation one day. "I had my marijuana, my women; I didn't have to work. And then y'all showed up," he said, chuckling.

Twiggy soon discovered that our presence actually enhanced his summer with the ladies. He'd casually mention to the women he dated that he had rescued his poor, bedraggled little brothers from the evil clutches of a foster home. Then he'd introduce us to them when he brought them home at night.

"It worked out good," he told me later, laughing. "Women love that sensitivity. They can't resist. I never went wrong."

That was the last time Patrick and I ever set foot in a foster home. I never said goodbye to Aunt Fannie. And I never heard from her again.

But running away from my whiteness—now, that was more difficult. My father made sure of that.

While he was overseas, word had gotten back to him about our great escape. Three months later, he came home from South America with another late-night surprise.

It was about three in the morning when I heard rustling at the front door. I went downstairs to see my father hauling in his familiar green duffel bag. This time, he had company.

A young white woman with long, stringy black hair and freckles stood next to my father. She was accompanied by a little white girl with a Prince Valiant haircut who looked no older than five. The woman greeted me with a stiff smile. I looked at her and then at my father.

"This is your new mother," he said gruffly as he dragged his bag into the house.

I looked at Patrick, who had also come downstairs, alarmed and confused. *This must be a joke,* I thought.

My father had finally found us a mother, but it wasn't the one we'd been wondering about all our lives.

I looked down at the little girl and muttered a greeting. She tilted her head in confusion and said, "Qué?"

My new mother and sister didn't speak a word of English.

The woman's name was Margo. She and her young daughter,

Luz, came from an impoverished community in Valdivia, a town in southern Chile. This twenty-six-year-old Chilean was now supposed to navigate language and cultural barriers to raise two adolescent boys she'd never met before. And we were supposed to accept her and Luz as family while my father continued sailing.

When I asked my father how he'd made that decision, he shrugged. He said he'd been out drinking one night in Chile when he stopped at a restaurant to use the bathroom. As he was leaving, he spotted Margo doing dishes in the kitchen.

"She reminded me of another white girl I knew long ago," he said, referring to someone he'd met long before my mother. "I was always interested in Spanish, and I thought perhaps she could teach you all Spanish."

Margo didn't teach me Spanish, but through her I learned something about myself that would later fill me with shame. I treated her the same way that some Black people in my neighborhood treated me: as the enemy solely because of her light skin.

I saw Margo as an intruder, not as a family member. I wouldn't talk to her or Luz at the kitchen table. And I made no effort to help my new stepsister adjust to an alien culture and language when other kids picked on her and called her "white girl."

I wouldn't walk alongside Margo or Luz in public. I lagged behind them or walked in front of them to signal to everybody in my neighborhood that I wasn't with *them*—you know, those two white people.

Margo wasn't white in the American sense. She was a descendant of the Europeans who colonized Central and South America starting in the sixteenth century. She was a Latina who looked white. Those subtleties, though, were lost on me at age twelve.

Once when I was walking to the shopping center with Margo,

a group of my friends approached. One of them looked at me and Margo.

"That your mom, John?"

"No," I spat out within earshot of Margo. "That white lady ain't my mother."

I didn't bother to look at Margo to see how my words affected her. I didn't care. She was the color of the enemy. She reminded me of what I wanted to forget—to hide—about myself.

I couldn't seem to escape whiteness, no matter how hard I tried. Nor could I get past the encounter with whiteness that I never forgot: the white intruder or apparition—or whatever it was—that appeared in my childhood bedroom years earlier. I couldn't get that out of my mind, or what happened the morning after.

I'd kept a stack of birthday cards in a manila folder tucked in my dresser drawer. These were birthday cards mailed to me by my aunts and uncles. When I opened the drawer that morning, I noticed that the folder had been opened. About four of my cards were missing. Had he taken them? Why?

The missing cards just added more questions. Why would he frighten two boys? Was he some kind of monster? And why would he leave footprints?

I instinctively realized that these were clues to a mystery—and that I would have to solve it one day.

CHAPTER 3

Can I Get a Witness?

Aunt Sylvia

A missing mother, foster homes, and a terrifying nocturnal visit. It might seem like my childhood was one miserable episode after another.

But my early years unfolded along two parallel tracks. There was turmoil. And then there was Aunt Sylvia, my father's younger sister. She watched Pat and me every weekend at my father's house starting when I was about three.

She was much more than an aunt. She was our lifeline. And

our drillmaster. And while many of my days were filled with sadness and uncertainty, there was one constant.

Every Sunday morning began like this.

It was 10:30 A.M., and I was a pouting eight-year-old sitting in the kitchen, poking through my Frosted Flakes. Sunlight streamed through the window, a sparkling new *Sgt. Rock* comic book rested on the table beside me, and the morning matinee *Son of Frankenstein* was about to come on TV.

But I knew that all these delectable Sunday morning diversions would soon be taken away from me.

The phone on the kitchen wall rang. I picked it up and heard the husky, breathless voice of Aunt Sylvia say, "I'm coming over. Be ready." Then, after a pause, she added, "Don't *make* me come in that house to get you."

I rolled my eyes, hung up, and walked to the front door to keep a lookout. Pat shuffled behind me, yawning. I was dressed in an itchy beige three-piece polyester suit with a clip-on tie; he was sporting a light-gray suit with a thick black tie slightly askew. Fifteen minutes later, we heard a car horn outside. I parted the living room curtains and saw a baby-blue Chevy Impala double-parked out front. We hustled out and climbed into the car just before it took off, gospel music blasting.

I fidgeted in the back seat and watched my buddies on the sidewalk, laughing and joking as they bounced down the street with bats and gloves. One of them spotted me as we drove by and gave me a taunting grin. I sank deeper into my seat and sulked. I had four hours of church service ahead of me.

Aunt Sylvia quit a secretarial job in New York City and moved to Baltimore to help raise us. No matter how uncertain life became for Pat and me, she was there to pick us up. She was our lighthouse in a sea of chaos.

She was a diminutive woman with a rich, dark complexion who loved to throw her head back and laugh loudly while clapping her hands. She wore a short, curly black wig, white gloves, and bright wide-brimmed hats to church. She wasn't big on physical affection; instead, she expressed love through her attention to details. She took Pat and me to doctor's appointments, enrolled us in Head Start programs, purchased our school clothes—no need of ours seemed to escape her notice.

There were no mushy stewed tomatoes for dinner when she cooked. She made big, down-home meals: spicy fried chicken that tasted good even when it was cold, baked ham, macaroni and cheese, and homemade biscuits glazed with butter. Her cakes and pies were addictive. So much so that they rarely survived a day. She boasted that all her desserts were made from scratch. To her, any baker who used pre-mixed ingredients was a fraud.

Since everybody had a nickname in my family, she gave me mine: "Repeating John." If she asked me to do anything, I had to know why.

"Time to take a bath, John."

"Bath? Why I gotta take a bath?"

"I want you to sweep Miss Martha's porch."

"Sweep another porch? Why I gotta do that? I'm not related to her."

Aunt Sylvia wasn't ordained, but Patrick and I were her congregation. She constantly preached to us. The subtext of her sermons was the same: Don't be like your daddy.

She called him "Baldy on the Racetrack." Maybe she gave him that nickname because he took so many risks. She determined that Pat and I were going to be different. Dad was a rough, ill-mannered seaman; Pat and I would be gentlemen. She became an ebony version of the columnist Miss Manners, drilling us on taste and refinement.

"Never walk down a street eating a sandwich; that's country."

"Being poor is no excuse for being dirty."

"Always open a door for a lady."

Her favorite subject, though, was Jesus. Aunt Sylvia didn't just talk to Jesus; she had him on speed dial. She broadcast songs about Jesus in a loud voice when she walked us through dimly lit areas of our neighborhood at night, because she thought gospel hymns warded off would-be muggers. She talked to Jesus while cooking, hanging laundry, and steering her big Impala nervously through stormy weather, her legs barely able to reach the pedals.

The subject of her prayers was usually my future and Pat's. I'd hear her talking to Jesus as I drifted off to sleep during long car rides.

"Lord, I just want to live long enough so that my boys will be okay."

"Lord, I just want them to grow up to be good men."

"Lord, I just want to live long enough to see them graduate from college, and then I know my work will be done."

She was a single woman in her thirties when she started watching us part-time. I never knew why we couldn't live with her, and I never thought to ask. She never married, had no children. She kept a man's tie and a pair of men's shoes in her bedroom, but my relatives thought those objects were a bluff. We never saw her with a man.

Before she could afford to buy a car, we took the bus or walked everywhere. When the three of us trudged together through those cold, drab streets in West Baltimore at night, it was us against the world. She introduced us as "my boys." I told teachers that she was my mother and put her name in the box labeled "mother" on school forms.

I never asked Aunt Sylvia about my actual mother. And she never volunteered any information, aside from giving one tantalizing clue to Patrick: She told him that one of our mother's relatives called us "zebra children."

I craved her approval like a flower bends toward the sunlight. When I showed her my report card, she'd lower her head, take her glasses off, and study the grades in silence. She'd raise her head and solemnly look at me, and suddenly her dark face would light up with a smile, a smile that made me feel like I'd been wrapped in a warm blanket.

I needed all the warmth I could get. Baltimore winters were brutal. We often ran out of money for food and heating oil as temperatures dipped into the teens. My father's checks from overseas were routinely late or didn't come at all. And Aunt Sylvia never made enough from her job as a public high school secretary to consistently pay for heat.

One winter night when I was about ten was one of the worst. We ran out of heating oil while we were at Aunt Sylvia's for the weekend. Aunt Sylvia placed rickety portable heaters in our bedroom, but I could still hear Patrick's teeth chattering when she left the room. We shivered under our blankets for what seemed like hours until she returned. She pulled our winter coats from the closet and draped them over us. Then she looked at us silently while we continued to shiver.

She turned around and went downstairs to the kitchen, where she boiled water and poured it into jars. She returned to our room with the jars and nestled them under our winter coats to help warm us. When the jars cooled, she returned to our bedroom and took them downstairs to boil the water again. She continued to march up and down the stairs for hours to make sure we stayed warm.

Pat's teeth finally stopped chattering and he fell asleep. The last sounds I heard that night as I drifted off to sleep were her footsteps, still going up and down the stairs.

She had a way of warming our spirits too. On another dreary winter evening, we were moping around, anticipating our return to the foster home the following day. She summoned us to the upstairs hallway and told us to wait. A playful smile flickered across her face.

She went into her bedroom and pulled a brown portable record player from her closet. She plugged it in and put on a vinyl record. A burst of marching band music filled the house. I looked at Patrick in confusion. Aunt Sylvia then took two sheets of newspaper, folded them into band hats, and placed them on our heads.

"Get behind me, boys!" she shouted as she herded us behind her considerable hips. "Let's march!"

As the band music swelled, Aunt Sylvia high-stepped up and down the hallway like a drum major. We stumbled behind her, trying to keep up.

"You're going too fast!" I yelled over the music.

"You're young—keep up," she said.

As soon as we were able to match her stride, she pirouetted at the end of the hall and showed us how to high-step and swing our arms in unison. We kept tripping over ourselves trying to match her steps. All three of us were laughing by the time the music ended.

"Let's do it again!" I said, sprawled on the floor, trying to catch my breath.

And we did.

When I went to bed that night, I was still smiling as she tucked me in.

Aunt Sylvia gave me another gift—a pair of wings to escape the misery of foster homes. She introduced me to books. We couldn't afford to buy them, but she would bring home second-hand books from the public schools where she worked and pile them on the dining room table. She challenged me with quizzes about what I read, bragged to relatives about how smart I was, and once even took me on a Greyhound bus to visit Gettysburg National Military Park in Pennsylvania after she saw me obsessively reading about the Civil War.

This love wasn't unconditional; it came with a price. We had to get what Aunt Sylvia called "training." We had to go to church with her every—and I mean *every*—Sunday. We couldn't even get out of church attendance when our father returned home. She left my father's house for her own place when he returned from overseas, but she made sure to still pick us up every Sunday.

My father had his own Sunday morning ritual. It involved making pancakes, watching black-and-white Westerns on TV, and snoring on the living room sofa. He never went to church.

We'd frequently pass him on our way out the front door and see him lounging on the sofa, Sunday newspaper spread on the coffee table before him.

"Dad, why we gotta go to church?" I asked him on one occasion. "You don't go to church. Why can't we stay home with you?"

"You do what Aunt Sylvia says," he gruffly replied without taking his eyes off the TV.

Even my father didn't dare cross Aunt Sylvia. She'd constantly march into the house to chide him about not providing her with enough money to pay the bills and buy us food and clothes. She was barely five feet, but my father wouldn't try to argue when Aunt Sylvia got in his face.

"He was like a little boy," Pat said recently. "He wouldn't talk back. He'd have his head down. He couldn't look in her eyes."

"She was our champion," I agreed.

She never had to spank me or Pat. All it took was a stern look for me to shut up. I was too afraid to let her down.

The church she made us go to every Sunday was Union Temple Baptist Church, an all-Black congregation on North Avenue, the main artery that cuts through West Baltimore. It looked like a medieval castle: It was built on massive brownstone slabs and had heavy wooden doors and a bell tower. The sign out front read "Baptist," but it was actually a Pentecostal church where people believed in prophecies, call-and-response during sermons ("Tell it, Preacher!" "That's all right!" "Yesssssir!"), dancing in the aisles, and "getting happy"—an ecstatic celebration in which people lost themselves in frenzied celebrations during worship.

It was also a church full of hierarchies—each member had their designated place in worship. Many of Union Temple's church members were blue-collar people: janitors, itinerant carpenters, and mechanics. But come Sunday morning, they took on new identities. Sharply dressed ushers with white pocket squares and gloves marched with military precision down the aisles as they ushered visitors to designated pews. The nattily attired deacons had reserved seating in the front rows of the church, along with their wives, and they were the first to line up in front to receive communion. The choir members followed them. And God help the visitor who accidentally sat in the front row. Congregants would watch and murmur as an usher rushed to steer them politely but firmly to regular pews in the back, where the heathens sat.

The Reverend Dr. Charles H. Churn presided over Union Temple as our senior pastor. The congregation treated him as if he were just a step below God. He was a handsome man with a cinnamon complexion, a square jaw, and a neatly cropped silver Afro. Draped in a billowy burgundy robe, he sat like a king in an enormous wooden chair that looked more like a throne—it sat higher than the two other pulpit chairs, which held assistant pastors. He was an old-style preacher who whooped, sweated, and shouted through his sermons, punctuating them with remarks like "Can I get a witness?" and "You don't know what I'm talking about!"

I was fascinated by what Reverend Churn drove, not what he said. It sat in a reserved parking space in front of the church: a gold-and-brown Rolls-Royce, complete with a water fountain nestled in the dashboard. God was indeed good.

Sunday morning worship, though, was bad—bad as in boring, achingly dull. My mood during service shifted between boredom, confusion, and contempt. I thought people getting happy were acting like buffoons. And I couldn't stand hearing Reverend Churn shout so much during sermons. When I was a kid, I thought he shouted more when people didn't put enough in the offering plate. I tuned him out by placing history books in my lap and pretending I was consulting Scripture while he preached.

Still, there were mysterious moments of undeniable power in worship—moments that would make more sense to me when I became older. One happened when I was about fifteen. It was revival night, an evening service that was more informal than Sunday morning worship. We were all packed into Union Temple's sanctuary, facing the pulpit and a huge portrait of a white, blond, blue-eyed Jesus praying in the Garden of Gethsemane. I was sitting in the back alone, a sullen teenager sneaking looks at a book on World War II, when something happened.

It began with one of the choirs. They were supposed to end their song after four verses, but they'd caught fire and kept going. Some church members stood and started clapping along while shouting, "Yes, Lord!" An elderly woman screamed, and then she shot upright out of her pew and started flailing her arms. More people stood up, swaying in the pews while clapping and stomping their feet.

As the frenzy intensified, a wave of heat seemed to ripple through the congregation. I could feel it heading my way.

A guy in a nearby pew who routinely slept through services threw up his arms and shouted. I got hot under the collar and started to sweat. *What's going on?* I wondered.

Something slipped inside me. I felt a tingling sensation. An electrical current was racing up my spine toward my mouth. I watched myself drop the book I was reading. I watched myself stand up—even though I didn't want to. I no longer had control over my body. Something was surging through it. I was about to clap, scream—I didn't know what I was about to do.

I scooted out of my pew and raced to the church's exit. I shoved the heavy wooden front door open and sighed with relief as I inhaled the cold night air. I started walking around the block, listening to cars swish by. The tingling sensation left. I returned to find that everyone had settled back into their pews. Parishioners were fanning themselves with a look of contentment on their faces, shouting, "Thank you, Jesus!" while others bowed their heads and sniffled in their seats. I sat down, found my page in my history book, and resumed reading.

There was, however, one part of church that I actually liked. It was a Black church tradition called "testimony time." It took place on the second Sunday evening of every month, when the church observed communion. This tradition was another church moment that would take on deeper significance when I became older.

One evening captured for me the hypnotic power of testimony time. The choir sang a series of slow spirituals in a hushed, chant-like rhythm as people in the pews closed their eyes and swayed in their seats. Then the choir sat down, and the congregation became silent. Deacon Johnson, a retired Pullman porter who had lost two fingers on his right hand in a railway accident, was the first to stand up near the front of the church, facing the pulpit, and give his testimony. "Giving honor to God, I want to tell the church about how good God has been to me this week," he said as he folded his hands in front of him, covering his missing fingers. He then told the church how he had gotten through an illness. People nodded silently in sympathy. He sat down with a smile on his face and mouthed a quiet prayer.

Then another woman stood up near the back of the church, an anxious look on her face. "I want to ask the church for prayers for my son. He's a good boy, but now he's hanging out with the wrong crowd."

And so it went all night—people standing up at random, with no prompting, to share their joys and sorrows.

Outside, twilight was approaching. The sun was setting on the other side of the stained-glass windows, and the evening shadows were starting to lengthen across the sidewalk. The hum of street traffic had ebbed; people were heading home to get ready for another workweek.

Yet inside the church, it felt like we had all the time in the world. Speaker after speaker stood to share the most intimate details of their lives, and no one seemed to judge. Parishioners encouraged speakers with shouts of "My, my!" or "It's all right!" It seemed as if everyone were reaching out with unseen hands and encircling each speaker with an invisible hug.

We were people who couldn't afford therapy. Church was our catharsis. Singing, shouting, and sharing stories gave us the strength to, as Reverend Churn liked to say, "make a way out of no way." We worshipped much like our ancestors did during slavery. Our worship was fervent, almost desperate. Hearing those spirituals made me feel as if the ghosts of enslaved Africans entered the church. The only white person I ever saw in my church was the rendering of Jesus that hung on the wall behind the pulpit. If any white person had visited, I'm not sure they would have felt at home. This was a different kind of Christianity from that of the staid and stiff white churches I sometimes saw on TV. In classic Black church worship, you were *supposed* to lose control of your emotions and body. The theologian James Cone often said that the God of the people who are riding on the deck of the slave ship is not the God of the people who are riding underneath the deck as slaves in chains.

Aunt Sylvia didn't just introduce us to a church community; she connected us to our family. She took us to just about every weekend family outing during our youth. My father's family was big. There were five brothers and four sisters. And they, along with my assorted cousins, nieces, and nephews, were loud. During summer cookouts, I watched my aunts and uncles spread newspaper across picnic tables in the backyard to eat crabs and swap jokes. When the sun set, they'd go into the house, where the family would stage a dance-off in the basement while blasting R&B groups like the Spinners and Earth, Wind & Fire from the stereo.

All my aunts and uncles were born in a segregated America. None went to college or had access to professional jobs. Some went into the military: Two of my uncles were combat veterans from World War II. Others found a foothold in the middle class through working in public schools, working as a nurse, or—one of the most coveted jobs—working as a mailman for the United States Postal Service as my uncle "Rock" Williams did. Many rolled up to our family dinners in style: getting out of shiny new cars like the Pontiac LeMans or the Oldsmobile Cutlass Supreme, with pine tree scents swinging on the rearview mirror and gleaming leather seats still smelling new.

They were members of unions, churches, the NAACP, the National Guard, and fraternal groups like the Freemasons. They all lived within five square miles of one another. They bickered, feuded, and barged unannounced into one another's homes; even as a kid I could tell they loved one another.

The family get-togethers would end with movie time. Uncle John, a church deacon and World War II veteran who had a portable camera, would summon everyone into the living room and click on a loud projector that would show home movies of our family. In those shaky movies, I'd see two pale boys with parted hair laughing and running among a sea of Black faces at some family outing or other. Yet no one ever mentioned that we were half-white, or anything about our mother.

I'd reminisce with Pat years later about what those family outings meant to us. "We were considered white boys, outcasts, the lowest of the low in Baltimore, by people who didn't know us," Pat said. "But we felt utterly embraced, accepted, and loved by our mom's family."

We had extended family in West Baltimore that looked out for us as well: Little League coaches, teachers who encouraged me to write, a tennis coach who taught me discipline. Some of these helpers were white teachers. One elementary school teacher, a tiny, bowlegged Jewish woman named Judith Sheinbrock, discovered I had a love of history. She took me and three other classmates on a train to Washington one weekend to visit the Smithsonian National Museum of Natural History.

It never occurred to me that there might be more white people like Mrs. Sheinbrock. I saw her as an exception, not like the rest.

But what happens when a troubled kid doesn't have an Aunt Sylvia? What happens when something goes wrong for that kid and it's too late for an adult to step in?

That was also a story I knew all too well, because it had happened in my own family, to one of the boys I played with in those home movies.

His name was Michael Edward Brown, Jr., and he was my nephew, the son of my half sister, Stephanie, whom we all called Lenny.

But Mike was more like a brother to Pat and me. We did everything together as kids: played pickup baseball games in the streets, popped wheelies on our rickety bikes, and stayed up late on Saturday nights to watch Elvis Presley movies. Mike was a smart, playful, athletic kid with a short-cropped Afro and a laid-back, confident air. His nickname was "Bambsy."

We all became teenagers together: me, Pat, Mike, and his older brother, Mark. We were the Four Amigos, always hanging out, walking to each other's houses at night, staying close as we became young men.

One winter night when he was about sixteen, Pat decided to visit Mike at his grandmother's apartment in West Baltimore. As

Pat approached the front door, he froze. There was a body on the sidewalk, its face partially covered by a thick winter coat. It was the body of a Black teenager who was around the same age as Mike, with the same build and haircut and the same Reebok tennis shoes.

Pat's heart started to race as he walked toward the apartment. *Oh Lord. I hope this isn't Mike*, he thought.

Several uniformed police officers stood next to the body, shivering, their breath forming a misty cloud in the frigid air. The teenager had just been shot to death; they hadn't yet had time to cordon the area with yellow crime-scene tape.

One of the officers turned to look at Pat, tilting his head in curiosity after noticing the look of dread on Pat's face. He nodded in the direction of the body. "Do you know him?" he asked. He stooped and flicked the jacket away from the teenager's face. There was a golf-ball-sized hole where the left eye had been, with hardly a trickle of blood visible. The teenager lay on his side as if he were taking a nap.

Pat edged closer to look at the body. He let out a deep sigh and looked at the officer. "Naw, I don't know him," he said, shaking his head.

Mike had escaped that night, but he'd already seen more than any kid should. He saw his father, Michael Sr., beat and stab his mother. My sister, Lenny, had shoulder-length hair, a caramel complexion, and high cheekbones dotted with freckles. She was as loud as she was pretty—always laughing and making up nicknames for family members. One summer day when I was with Mike, who was about ten, we saw worse. I was staying with Lenny when she began arguing with her husband. He ran Mike and me out of the house and locked the doors so we wouldn't intervene.

We heard Lenny scream from inside. We ran to a window and peered through a white cotton curtain, glimpsing my sister raising her hands to shield herself and seeing another hand gripping a kitchen knife. The white curtain was suddenly sprayed by my sister's blood. Mike and I ran to a neighbor's house and asked them to call the police.

Lenny survived the stabbing with only a wound to her hand, but her marriage crumbled. Mike's father disappeared and soon after died of a heroin overdose. Mike eventually moved in with his grandmother, but she was too old and too frail to keep up with him. He had no Aunt Sylvia to encourage him to do well in school, so he dropped out of high school. He had no father to discipline him, so he drifted into crime: vandalism, then smoking weed and dealing drugs. He became a forerunner of Omar, the shotgun-wielding character who robbed drug dealers on the HBO series *The Wire*. But there was no Hollywood glamour in trying to make a living that way. He was shot in the buttocks while trying to rob a drug dealer. Not long after, his grandmother died and he became homeless. Mike was eventually jailed for dealing drugs. His life was one tragic falling domino after another.

The final domino fell on another winter night. By now Mike was a married man, with a daughter, Stephanie, named after his mother, and a son, Michael Jr. Pat had gone to see Mike that night. When he got to the house, he saw double-parked police cars with flashing lights and squawking radios. Yellow tape with the warning "Crime Scene Do Not Cross" was plastered across Mike's front door.

Oh God, Pat thought as he walked toward Mike's house.

Mike had overdosed, having snorted a mixture of heroin and cocaine, a dangerous practice known as "speedballing." He had robbed a drug dealer earlier that night. His ten-year-old daughter had found her father crouched on his knees with his head slumped in the toilet, clenching a plastic lighter in his left hand, dried blood crusted around his nose.

"I just miss the love I used to feel from him," Pat said one evening as we reminisced about Mike, talking about all the times we played together as kids and spent the night at each other's houses.

"So do I, Pat," I said. "So do I. . . ."

West Baltimore hadn't earned its notorious reputation when Mike and I were teenagers in the 1980s. *The Wire* was still decades away. No American president had yet declared that West Baltimore was "the Worst in the USA," a "filthy place" where "no human being would want to live."[1] Yet by the time I reached high school, virtually all my friends had stories like mine to tell. We all seemed to know a Mike, someone who got swept away by the drugs and the violence.

As I became a pre-teen, questions about my racial identity took a back seat to a more immediate concern: navigating the violence and drugs swirling around me. I attended one of the most dangerous public schools in Baltimore: William H. Lemmel Junior High. No one dared walk to or from school alone; you stayed in groups for safety. There were constant fights; several of my classmates were stabbed, and student riots shut down school on several occasions. When a local television crew showed up to cover one riot, they were robbed.

The violence in my neighborhood escalated as the years passed. My best friend's sister was murdered by a serial killer. One of my close friends strangled a woman and stole her VCR. And another young man I knew tortured and murdered a boy because the boy's older sister wouldn't go out on a date with him. That murder made the front page of the local newspaper.

More headlines would follow as crack cocaine hit Baltimore. Commentators started describing young Black men from inner-city neighborhoods like mine as "superpredators."[2] Others warned of an epidemic of "crack babies."[3] And one conservative columnist said crack was creating a "bio-underclass," a generation of damaged inner-city babies "whose biological inferiority is stamped at birth."[4]

My neighborhood didn't even sound the same anymore. The young men who sang Motown classics in front of the corner store on my block disappeared. That happened not long after someone robbed the store's owner and shot him in the face. The Arabbers, the Black fruit vendors who used to pull clanking horse-drawn carts up the streets while calling out their prices, vanished. Another sound replaced their voices: the steady *whomp-whomp* of police helicopters hovering over our block.

I could cross the street to avoid a dangerous person. I could steer clear of drugs when I saw what was happening to Mike and what alcohol did to my father. And I always had Aunt Sylvia in my corner, telling me I could do anything. Yet I experienced another type of violence that still haunts me. It was a type of violence that broke spirits, not bodies. It was insidious because it didn't grab headlines or lead to HBO shows. By the time I became a teenager, I had absorbed the belief—born out of this violence—that I wasn't as smart as white people.

I didn't know that I had become its victim until a teacher, Cheryl Pasteur, approached me in my senior year with a request.

Mrs. Pasteur was an English teacher who also taught drama.

She was a young, effervescent woman with bronze skin, dimples, and hoop earrings, and she loved to praise students. I was leaving her class one day when she ran up behind me and caught me in the hallway. "Mister Blake, Mister Blake," she said, stringing out the word *Mister* in a playful greeting. "I have something special for you."

I turned to see her smile and announce with great fanfare, "You've been invited to join *It's Academic*."

My smile vanished. My head started to spin. "Oh, that's great," I stammered before she cut me off.

"We start practices this weekend. Can you . . ."

I didn't hear what else she said because I was envisioning getting embarrassed on television. *It's Academic* was a local television quiz show that featured three teams of the smartest public and private high school students from Baltimore, all nominated by teachers because of their grades and ability. The three-member teams faced off against one another every Saturday morning on a local television station, where a host fired a range of academic questions at them. I occasionally watched the show on Saturday morning and only ever saw preppy white kids from posh suburban schools competing.

Mrs. Pasteur tilted her head and looked at me with concern. "You can do this, John," she assured me. "I've told you this before: We expect great things from you."

Great things? I thought. *Who expects great things from me?*

"Ah, can I think about it?" I asked.

"Of course you can," she said, smiling brightly again. "Let me know by tomorrow."

I lowered my head as I walked away, ignoring the bustle in the hallway as the bell rang. I already knew what my answer would be. When I told Mrs. Pasteur the next day that I couldn't do it, her brow furrowed in confusion. She gave me a tight smile and walked away.

I sighed with relief.

I never saw anybody who looked like me on *It's Academic*. I never heard anyone say anything good about West Baltimore in newspapers or on television—or about the young Black men like me who lived there. We were "super-predators," part of the "bio-underclass," poor Black people with no future. You hear a story repeated enough, and you start believing it.

I saw so many dreams murdered before they could take flight. My classmates talked about becoming lawyers, business executives, and doctors. That kind of talk evaporated by the time we reached high school, as many of us shifted our expectations to going into the military or learning a trade. I thought I'd end up working a minimum-wage job in a warehouse after high school or going into the U.S. Marines. I couldn't imagine graduating from college or going to work in a suit and tie, even though my brother Twiggy had done so.

I never got into trouble with the law. But I could have on several occasions, particularly when I was in junior high. During one fight, I smashed another teenager's head with a rock, leaving his blood splattered on the pavement. He survived, but what if he had died?

I occasionally walked to a railroad bridge overlooking Gwynns Falls Parkway, the picturesque route I had used to run away from Aunt Fannie's. I'd stand on the bridge and throw rocks at the cars passing below. I was bored and angry; I wanted to crack a windshield or cause a crash. Fortunately, my aim was as bad as my intention, but what if I had sent someone to the hospital or worse?

There was little margin for error for young men from West

Baltimore. Mike fought like hell to live a better life when he became a man. He worked two, sometimes three jobs to support his wife and two kids. He rode his bright-orange mountain bike to work when he lost his license because of drunk driving. He joined a church and got baptized, and was overjoyed when Pat showed up for the ceremony. He got together with Pat in parking lots after work to talk about getting off drugs.

"It's hard, Unc," he'd tell Pat. "I'm trying. I know I need to get in a program."

He never got over losing both of his parents when he was thirteen. There was no Aunt Sylvia to swoop in and save the day. Twiggy invited Mike and his brother, Mark, to live with him when both reached high school. Twiggy lived in a comfortable suburban home in Silver Spring, Maryland. For a time, Mike and Mark went to good schools and were on the verge of escaping West Baltimore. But they missed living in their old neighborhood and being around their friends, so they opted to return to their grandmother, who lived in a rough neighborhood where crime and drugs were commonplace. Mike preferred the familiar over the new even if he knew that life with Twiggy would offer him a better future.

I had something else that Mike didn't—a father. He may have been there only three or so months out of the year, but he was there.

Still, by the time I became a teenager, my bond with my father was gone. He was no longer my hero. I'd gotten tired of the drinking, the partying, the brazen womanizing that continued even after his marriage to Margo. My hero had become an embarrassment, one I thought was worthy of my contempt.

He returned my contempt. I didn't fit his idea of a man. A real man worked with his hands around the house and chased women.

I could barely hold a hammer and was too shy to attend my school proms.

When I was in high school, I failed another initiation into adulthood—my driving test. I returned home, crushed. My father asked me what had happened. When I told him, a look of disgust creased his face. "John, you don't know shit about shit," he said.

Our relationship deteriorated so much that he summoned the most despised group in our community—the police—to deal with me. He called the police on me at least three times during high school and kicked me out of the house for not "obeying" him. My infractions ranged from not properly sweeping the floor to not being upstairs promptly at "0600 hours to carry out my assigned duties": the laundry list of chores he assigned every Saturday morning.

If I complained, he'd point to a placard that he had hung on his bedroom door. It read "Captain."

"There can only be one captain on a ship," he said. "If you don't like it, you can get the hell out."

I didn't realize how much bitterness I carried against my father until my senior year in high school. I made the discovery during another "Ramblin' Rose" night.

I heard his Bronco pull up outside as I sat on the couch in the living room. As he fumbled for his keys, I shook my head, got up, and opened the door. He was staggering to keep upright.

Drunk again, I thought. *When is it ever going to end?*

I placed his right arm over my shoulders and half carried, half dragged him inside while he muttered something I couldn't understand.

As I steered him through the living room, past the coffee table littered with ashtrays and beer cans, a choking sound escaped my throat. My eyes started to water and I burst into tears.

I stifled my sobs, so shocked by them that I almost dropped my father.

Where were you when I was in those foster homes and needed you to carry me? I thought as I propped him up. *Where were you when I wanted to learn about my mother?*

"The son is supposed to lean on the father, not the other way around," I whispered, hoping he couldn't hear me.

He started coughing, and his eyes closed as his head slumped to his chest. As his body sagged, I guided him into his bedroom. I eased him onto his bed, lifted his Baltimore Orioles baseball cap off his head, and placed his feet on the bed. He started snoring.

I took a final look, then turned and quietly closed the door.

By this time, I had also closed the door on my mother. I occasionally thought about her, but I stopped asking any questions. The other relatives on my mother's side didn't even cross my mind. *If I have a future,* I thought, *it will only be as a Black man.*

Then, one afternoon during my senior year in high school, I heard my father call from his bedroom, "John, come here!"

I opened his bedroom door. He was in his customary spot: sitting upright and shirtless in bed, his Buddha belly spilling over his waistband as he watched *The Price Is Right.* He turned his eyes from the show and surveyed me with a curious, searching expression. Then he nonchalantly asked, "Do you want to meet your mother?"

I was too stunned to say anything in response. I just stared at him with my mouth open as *The Price Is Right*'s studio audience erupted in giddy applause.

CHAPTER 4

The Patron Saint of Hopeless Causes

Pat (left) and John with their mother, Shirley Dailey

walked into a large waiting room with fluorescent lighting, mustard-colored walls, and a wobbly coffee table with musty *Reader's Digest* magazines scattered on top. Pat followed in silence. We sat down on a dingy beige plastic-upholstered couch with ripped seams and scanned our drab surroundings, fidgeting in our seats.

I straightened my collar. I had worn my favorite outfit, a thick beige cotton sweater with a new navy-blue polo shirt. I was seventeen, Pat a year younger. I picked up a *Reader's Digest* to scan the cover, but inside I was churning with questions: *What does she look like? Am I supposed to call her Mom? Why now?*

My father may have extended the invitation, but he was absent. After dropping his bombshell of a question, he left in the middle of the night for a sailing trip to South America. My sister, Lenny, had volunteered to drive us to see our mother. She led us into the large room and leaned against a wall after we sat down. She said nothing, which was uncharacteristic. My palms started to sweat.

Pat caught sight of someone moving in an adjoining hallway. His eyes narrowed. Then he leaned forward before standing and craning his neck.

I followed his gaze and spotted a thin white woman in baggy clothes. She was taking long loping strides, but her arms remained rigid at her sides.

Wow, I thought. *That's just how Pat walks.*

I stood up next to Pat, watching the woman in silence.

Her gaze caught ours and she stopped. Her eyes widened, and a huge smile lit up her face. She started walking toward us.

Pat and I stood frozen next to each other. As she got closer, she broke into a shuffling trot and virtually fell into us with outstretched arms.

"Oh boy! Oh boy!" she said like a kid unwrapping a present on Christmas morning. "Hi, John. Hi, Pat. It's so good to see you."

I took a step back as she reached for me. She quickly closed the space, and I gave her a stiff hug. She then looked up at Pat and embraced him. He smiled.

As she hugged Pat, I stepped back to look at my mom for the first time that I could remember. I opened my mouth to say something, but no words came out as I tried to take in what I was seeing.

How . . . Why . . . What happened to her? I wondered.

Her face was long and gaunt and devoid of makeup. She was thin as a needle—ninety-four pounds on a five-foot-seven frame—and her cheeks had the sunken look of someone who had already lost most of their teeth. She was thirty-six at the time but looked twenty years older. We wore the same type of beige knit sweater; hers, though, looked like a thrift-store donation, well-worn and peppered with lint.

Yet she had stunning, warm pale-blue eyes—they reminded me of the blue sky I had squinted up at as a kid during my kite-flying interlude.

"Oh, you're such handsome boys," she said in the working-class Baltimorean accent (for example, "Bawelmer" instead of "Baltimore") that was used only in the white working-class sections of Baltimore where few Blacks dared to go. She couldn't stop smiling, and she kept staring at us, shaking her head in disbelief that we were actually there.

I didn't share her joy.

As she talked to Pat, I stepped back to collect myself and take in more of my surroundings. I was standing in one room of a sprawling complex of dark redbrick buildings ringed by tall chain-link fences—a scene that looked like it could have been used as the set for the prison film *The Shawshank Redemption.* Someone moaned in agony in an adjacent room while another person erupted in hysterical laughter. A beefy Black man in a tight white uniform who had been walking alongside my mother had stepped back to watch our reunion, stifling a yawn. A whiff of ammonia and urine drifted through the waiting room.

I lowered my head and sighed. A wave of sadness and confusion came over me. *I waited all these years for this?*

I had finally found my mother, only to discover that most of her had already been lost.

My mother was a patient in a mental institution.

"Burying the lede" is an expression used in journalism. It means burying the most important information about a story deep in an article when it should have been placed at the opening. My dad's family didn't just bury the lede about my mother. They placed it in the footnotes. No one ever told Pat or me that our mother had a mental illness. I didn't even know that she was alive until I heard my father's invitation.

Still, I had already received hints that my first meeting with my mom wouldn't be a Hallmark moment. The first came from Lenny. At first, she said little after Pat and I climbed into her gray Toyota Celica that morning for the twenty-three-mile drive from West Baltimore to Crownsville. We drove in silence, passing liquor stores, storefront churches, and row houses before we finally entered rural Maryland, dotted with farms and country roads. I looked out the window, imagining what my mom would look like and what I would say.

Lenny finally broke the silence to say, "Now prepare yourself. Your mom is sick." She said nothing more and continued to grip the steering wheel, staring solemnly ahead.

Sick? What does that mean? I wondered. For once, I didn't ask any questions. I was too preoccupied.

It was ironic, though, that Lenny was the one taking me to see my mom. She was the only one in my family who had inadvertently given me a clue about my mother's condition before our meeting. About two years earlier, I was arguing with her during another car ride when she blurted out, "That's why you going to be crazy just like your mom, John."

Her words hit like an ice pick to my heart. I was too shocked to react. She never mentioned the comment again, and I didn't ask her what she meant.

A sign at the hospital's entrance gave me another clue. As Lenny pulled into the complex of colonial-style brick buildings arranged like military barracks, a sign read, "Crownsville Hospital Center. Your Community Behavioral Center Since 1911." The sign made little sense to me, though, because I didn't know how to parse the "community behavioral center" jargon.

And then while waiting for my mom inside the hospital, I saw something that should have removed all doubt. After Lenny parked in front and guided us to a waiting area, I was too nervous to stay seated. I rose and wandered to a nearby hallway, where I saw a series of closed steel doors with small rectangular windows. The hallway was empty, so I walked to a door and peeked in its window. An emaciated middle-aged white woman in a stained nightgown, stringy gray hair draped over her torso, was squatting in the middle of a dimly lit padded room. She sat frozen in the position, saying nothing as she stared at the wall. She didn't bother to acknowledge me as I watched her through the door's window. She looked like a tormented figure in a medieval painting, trapped in purgatory.

"You have to go back to the waiting room."

I jumped at the sound of the voice behind me. I turned to see another large Black man in a white uniform.

"What is she in there for?" I asked him, motioning toward the woman in the room.

"She killed her children," he said matter-of-factly. "Let's go," he said then, waving me toward the waiting room.

That encounter should have cleared up any mystery about my mom's condition. But the mind has ingenious ways of filtering out unwanted information. I ignored all these signs in addition to the moans and screams in the background. (I wouldn't remember them until more than twenty years later when Pat casually mentioned them to me while recalling the meeting.) I just didn't know how to accept all I was seeing and hearing.

I had no choice but to accept the awful truth, though, as I finally stared at my mom as she tried to hold a conversation with Pat. After he told her he liked photography, she said nothing and stared vacantly at him as if she were somewhere else.

Lenny nudged my shoulder. "John, tell her what you want to be when you grow up. Tell her about your schoolwork."

I recited my grade point average and said I wanted to be a journalist one day. My mom snapped back to look at me, her face lighting up with another smile. Pat said something that I don't remember. More awkward silence. Another vacant stare from my mom.

I clenched my jaw and pursed my lips. *This is so unfair,* I thought. *Nobody prepared us.* What was I supposed to feel? Was I supposed to call her Mom, cry out in joy? How could I feel anything for someone I had never met?

My mother, though, betrayed no nervousness. She leaned back on the couch and studied our faces with an easy smile. There was no trace of guilt, no offer of an explanation for her absence. As we talked more, her hand found mine. I stared in fascination as she held my hand, looking at the contrast between her bony, blue-veined hand and my brown one.

I slowly eased my hand out of hers and slid it under my thigh. She said nothing and continued beaming.

As we talked, it became clear that she had trouble following what I said. She kept repeating herself. She didn't ask us any questions about ourselves.

She lowered her voice to a conspiratorial whisper and leaned closer to me, asking me a series of questions.

"Can you get me some coffee and soda? I like Pepsi."

"Will you send me some money? I'm as poor as a church mouse."

"When are you going to see me again?"

I looked at Lenny.

"Soon," my sister said.

"For real?" my mom answered.

She then glanced over her shoulder to make sure no one was listening and whispered, "I'm scared. I don't want to be here."

My mom had reason to be afraid. Crownsville had a reputation for cruelty.[1] It was opened in 1911 to treat Black people who had mental illnesses. Many of its patients were chained to walls or strapped to chairs in windowless dorm rooms. Some were injected with malaria and hepatitis during medical experiments, while others were subjected to lobotomies and electroshock treatment. A local historian examining the site found the graves of at least 1,700 former patients whose final resting places were identified only by numbers.[2] No wonder the hospital was used as the setting for a horror movie after it closed down about twenty-five years after my first visit.[3]

But I didn't know any of Crownsville's history at the time. No one had prepared me. I said nothing. What could I say or do? It was too much to take in.

Pat started to talk. As Mom shifted her attention to him, I sneaked peeks at her face to see if I could find any traces of myself. There was something about her brow, cheekbones, and chin that looked familiar. Yet her accent and some of her mannerisms were alien to me. She was a stranger.

Lenny nudged me again. It was time to go.

Patrick had decided to document the occasion. He was a budding photographer. He took out his thirty-five-millimeter camera and told Mom that he wanted to take a picture. He motioned me back toward the couch. I sat down, followed by my mother, who sat to my right. She draped her left arm over my shoulder and looked at the camera with a contented smile. I folded my hands and held them in my lap.

Afterward I stood and gave Mom a mechanical hug. She looked at me and made a final request. "Will you send me a Saint Jude prayer book?"

"Ah yes, I will," I said, not knowing who Saint Jude is or anything about a prayer book.

I would find out later: Saint Jude is the patron saint of hopeless causes.

I don't remember much from the drive home. None of us talked. In fact, we never talked about Crownsville after that visit. We acted like it had never happened.

"We checked a box. We met our mom. We moved on," Pat said recently. "We already had a family, and we already had Aunt Sylvia, so there wasn't that void."

We would face a different void, though, not long after that meeting. Lenny died from a heart attack about seven months after taking us to Crownsville. She died on the eve of her wedding. Mike, who had such bad luck, was only thirteen at the time of his mother's death.

Before that tragedy struck, I kept thinking back to another surprise from that first meeting with my mom. It challenged one of my fundamental beliefs about race. As the horror of Crownsville began to sink in during that first meeting, I felt something toward my mother that I had never felt before toward any white person: pity. Watching my rail-thin mom try to string her thoughts together in her thrift-store clothes while people moaned in despair from nearby hallways, I thought, *I've never seen a Black person suffer like this.*

I thought we had a monopoly on suffering. I thought a white person couldn't understand what I, or any other person of color, went through—being ignored, misunderstood, and treated with contempt and brutality.

My mother crushed that assumption during our first meeting without saying a word.

I was still angry, but at my family. Why hadn't anyone told us about our mom before? Why hadn't anyone prepared us?

But Twiggy, as always, was there for me. I called him one night and asked him if there was some kind of family agreement to keep the truth from us.

He paused a long time, struggling to find the right words. "No, no, no," he finally said. "That's something that got lost in the shuffle. Dad was supposed to do that. There were certain things Dad didn't touch, and that might have been one of them."

Several weeks later, my father returned from South America. He had to talk now. I waited until he unpacked, then found him at the kitchen table, the place we normally talked about family business. I sat down while he was eating a steak.

"So, you finally met your mom, eh?" he said casually, looking at me with a smile.

I didn't think to ask why he hadn't been there. I knew by then that he didn't like any messy family drama. I was curious about something else.

"What's wrong with her, Dad?"

He dropped the fork. The smile vanished. He didn't look at me but stared straight ahead. He told me that my mother had schizophrenia, a blanket term describing one of the most severe forms of mental illness. People with schizophrenia often experience delusions, hallucinations, and catatonic states where they have difficulty expressing emotion. Many require lifelong treatment because they can't function in society. My mother had been in mental institutions for most of her life.

"Was she always like this?" I asked him. "How did she get this way?"

My father wiped his hands on a napkin, stood, and walked to a buffet in the dining room. He opened a drawer, grabbed a Ziploc bag, and returned to the kitchen. Not saying anything, he pulled a photograph out of the bag and pushed it toward me.

I picked up the photo and studied it. It was a black-and-white photograph of a twentyish white woman sitting at a kitchen table with a refrigerator in the background. She has a beehive hairdo and holds a cigarette in her right hand. Even though the photograph is sepia-toned and faded, it practically glows with her energy. She is looking at the camera with a wide, dimpled smile as if someone just told her a joke. Her gleaming eyes and exuberant smile light the frame.

I lowered the photograph and looked at my father. He had a half-eaten steak on his plate.

"Is this . . ."

"That's your mother," he said.

I scooted to the edge of my chair and studied the photograph again. Then I looked at my father. He lowered his head and half smiled as if he were recalling some happy memory. He began to tell me the story about what my mom was like when the photograph was taken—and how she had changed.

. . .

My father first spotted my mother in the cafeteria of the University of Maryland Medical Center in downtown Baltimore. Her name was Shirley Jean Dailey, and she was a nineteen-year-old nurse's assistant. He was a thirty-six-year-old divorcé with three teenage kids. He worked in the morgue between sailing trips to make extra money.

He approached and asked her out to lunch. She accepted.

It sounds simple, but it's hard to overstate how dangerous that brief exchange was for my dad. Interracial couples may be common today, but they certainly weren't in 1963, when my father invited my mom to lunch. There was hardly anything more risky a Black man could do during that time than ask a white woman out. Black men were routinely assaulted or killed for looking at a white woman the wrong way. Most Black people in my father's generation never forgot seeing the gruesome photos of Emmett Till's mutilated body in a coffin. Till was a fourteen-year-old Black boy who was murdered in Mississippi in 1955 for allegedly whistling at a white woman.[4]

The British singer Petula Clark sparked an international scandal when she *touched the arm* of Black singer and activist Harry Belafonte during a duet that aired on NBC.[5] A Black man courting a white woman bordered on a criminal act. Anti-miscegenation laws, which made interracial marriage illegal, were still on the books in Maryland and in other states.

Not only did my father ask my mother out, but he was also sixteen years older than my mom, who was still a teenager. It had all the ingredients for another scandal—or worse.

But my father wasn't one to shy away from risk. And, in fact, he did something even riskier. Not long after their first lunch date, he hailed a cab to her house.

"Where to?"

"2524 Wilkens Avenue," my father said as he slid into the back seat.

The cab driver, a Black man, did a double take and then turned to appraise my father.

"You sure you want to go there, partner?"

Wilkens Avenue was only 4.1 miles away from my father's house, but he might as well have been traveling to Mississippi. It was in one of the toughest white working-class neighborhoods in Baltimore, near the city's docks. The neighborhood was an all-white enclave of wide boulevards lined with trees, Catholic churches, and schools, a place where residents came out every Sunday morning to wash down the white marble steps of their row houses until they sparkled. Black people stayed away from Wilkens Avenue.

"Yeah, I'm sure," my father told the cabbie. "2524 Wilkens Avenue. Let's go."

The driver protested. They argued until my father negotiated a compromise. The driver would drop my father off one block away from the house.

My father stepped out of the cab and turned back to ask the cabbie to wait for him in case no one was home. The driver ignored him and took off.

My father walked to the front door of a row house that stood in the middle of a block so close to the city's docks that you could see ships on the horizon. He knocked. Silence. More knocking. The door cracked open. An elderly white man with thick salt-and-pepper hair brushed back from his face stole a peek at my father. Then he slammed the door shut without saying anything. My father kept knocking. A couple of minutes later, a Baltimore City police car pulled up to the house, and two white police officers emerged. As they started walking toward the house, the front door swung open and the man launched himself at my father, trying to shove him off the front steps.

"This nigger is trying to see my daughter," the man shouted to the police.

My father argued with the police about his rights. They responded by arresting him and taking him in for further questioning before releasing him that night.

That should have been the end of the story, but soon after, my mother did something unexpected: She paid a visit to my father at his house in West Baltimore. And she went back, again and again.

I would love to have seen the look on the face of whoever answered the door at my father's house when my mother first showed up, asking, "Is Clifton home?"

She became a regular, traveling the 4.1 miles from Wilkens Avenue to Pulaski Street in West Baltimore to go on dates with my father. She didn't just show up; she became part of the family, drawing double takes from Black people sitting on the stoops in my father's neighborhood as she strolled by. She often stayed over, sitting in the kitchen smoking cigarettes and talking to my grandmother Daisy Cora Lee Blake.

My grandmother was the matriarch of the family. She was a janitor at Frederick Douglass High School, the "colored" high school in West Baltimore, and a domestic who worked for white families. She was a soft-spoken woman who had grown up in the Jim Crow South, moving from North Carolina to Baltimore in the early twentieth century. Short, plump, and bowlegged, she usually wore a floral dress with an apron and spent most of her free time either reading the Bible on the front porch or singing gospel songs while baking cakes and homemade biscuits.

When I talked later to my older relatives who were there when my mother started visiting, they described someone who bore no resemblance to the fragile person I'd met at Crownsville. They said my mom was "happy-go-lucky," "witty," "jovial," someone who could command a room and reduce everyone to laughter with her jokes.

What most stood out was her utter ease around Black people. Our family couldn't understand it.

My cousin Howard, who we called "Reese," gave me a little more insight about my mother. Reese was a jovial U.S. Air Force veteran who spent much of his youth visiting my father's house to see my grandmother, so he was around my mother a lot.

"It was like a breakthrough," Reese told me. "She was a white woman on the block, not scared, not worried about being attacked, not looking over her shoulder. She didn't seem to be conscious of her color. She wasn't sitting in the corner wondering if she was going to fit in. She was like one of the family."

My brother Tony said the same. When my parents were dating, he was a teenager with a goatee, an Afro, and a lean body honed by hours in the gym as an amateur boxer. He was there for many of my mom's visits.

"If you would have told her that she was white, she would have said, 'What?'" Tony told me.

My mother eventually became particularly close to another person in my family, someone she would accompany on trips to the corner store and huddle with on the porch, laughing while sharing a private joke. That person was my sister, Lenny, who was also a teenager when my mother started visiting my father.

No wonder Lenny was the one who drove us to Crownsville to see our mother. She was the big sister Lenny never had.

Hearing all those stories puzzled me. Why was my mother so accepting of Black people? I pressed Tony on it, and like often

happened with members of my family, his voice rose in exasperation at hearing yet another one of my questions about race.

"Some people got their own mind," he said. "They don't buy
into that racism shit."

But my grandmother knew plenty of white people who bought
into racism. She constantly worried about my father, fretting that
his attraction to white women would get him beaten or killed.
After my mom left one day, my grandmother turned to my father
and asked, "How could you?"

My parents saw strangers in public who didn't bother to hide
their objections the way my grandmother did. My parents met
during the high-water mark of the Civil Rights Movement. The
Reverend Martin Luther King, Jr., delivered his "I Have a
Dream" speech during the same year they had their first lunch.
The nation would be transformed by the passage of two landmark laws—the 1964 Civil Rights Act and the 1965 Voting
Rights Act. But those changes took time to filter into ordinary
people's lives.

As my parents walked together through downtown Baltimore,
white drivers passing by would do a double take, make a U-turn,
and brazenly glare at them while slowly driving by. When my
father tried to hail a cab with my mother next to him, no one
would stop. One white cabbie locked the door, yelling, "Go get
a colored cab."

On numerous occasions, police officers approached my mother
while my father was at her side and asked, "Ma'am, is this man
bothering you?"

My father said he couldn't remember any time when my
mother expressed hesitation or fear about accompanying him in
public. "If it did bother her, she didn't show it."

On one of their dates, my father took my mother to one of the innumerable bars that sit on the corners in Baltimore. The one he chose was called Murphy's, a classic neighborhood tavern with a neon Pabst Blue Ribbon sign perched out front, framed pictures of local sports heroes like Baltimore Colts quarterback Johnny Unitas hanging on the wall inside, and working-class white men planted on oak barstools.

My father sidled up to the bar with my mother and ordered drinks. The bartender, a white man, scowled, then poured their drinks. After they finished their drinks, the bartender shattered their glasses behind the bar. My father ordered a second time. The bartender served them, then broke their empty glasses again.

"We got into a fight and tore that bar up," my father said. "We had to leave in a hurry."

At the time, I didn't ask my father what he meant by "we," but later I would find out.

The only public outing where they weren't harassed was after a national tragedy. After President John F. Kennedy was assassinated on November 22, 1963, they joined a crowd of 250,000 people who filed past Kennedy's flag-draped coffin in the Capitol Rotunda. Kennedy, the first Irish Catholic president of the United States, was a hero of my mother and of my father.

Even with all the answers I was given about my mother and her personality, I still couldn't wrap my head around why she was willing to take the risk and openly see a Black man at a time when it was taboo.

When I asked my father, he said, "I don't know why. I thought about it for a long time, and I could see it in her. She didn't see my color. She saw my character. I talked to one of her friends, and she told me that Shirley was open to people in general. It wasn't just Black people."

My mother's egalitarian spirit didn't run in the family. What her father did was bad enough. Not only did he physically assault my father while calling him the N-word, but he also put my father's life at risk by calling the police on him. White police officers had beaten and even killed Black men for lesser offenses in that era. My father was lucky to walk home after that visit. Once a white person calls the police on a Black person, all bets are off.

But another villain besides my mother's father emerged in these stories—my mother's younger sister, Mary Dailey. I had no photograph of her, but my father painted a portrait. He said she didn't like Black people—or me or Pat.

I never heard my father blame any personal misfortune on racism. He scoffed at Black people who became consumed by what he called "that racial stuff." He always looked for a reason other than racism to explain a white person's behavior. Not so with my mother's sister. He was blunt about how he thought she saw Black people—yet not too harsh because he was, after all, talking about my aunt.

"She didn't care for Blacks," my father said. "She wasn't all that happy to meet me. When we met, she kind of held back. We didn't say too much to each other."

Her silence said more to me than my father's words. She made no effort to contact Pat or me over the years. When I asked about it, my father's relatives told me that she didn't want anything to do with us because we were Black. I believed my mother's absence was justified because of her illness. I saw no reason to forgive Aunt Mary nor meet her. What could justify her rejection of her own nephews? I decided that I never wanted anything to do with her.

One of the most fascinating glimpses into my mom as a young woman came from a remark my brother Tony made. He was telling me about the time he watched my parents argue at my father's house, in front of my extended family. My father lobbed some kind of insult at my mother, and she responded with "Nigger!"

That story threw me. Did my mom really say that? What did people say?

When I asked Tony, he hesitated as if he hadn't meant to reveal that remark. Then reluctantly he said, "Everybody froze. I backed out of the room. I said to myself, *I'm too little to be hearing this.*"

Though I was initially afraid to ask my father, I kept wondering, Why would he go through so much to be with my mom? Was it lust, was it the allure of breaking a taboo, or was it because she was young and pretty? Maybe it was a combination of all of those.

But there were at least two other reasons he dared to knock on my mother's door on Wilkens Avenue in 1963. One came from a painful childhood event involving his father, the other from a remarkable social experiment that my father unwittingly participated in at sea.

My father never talked much about his father, John Arthur Blake. I knew that my grandfather was a diminutive man who would doff his hat and step off the sidewalk when white people approached. I heard one story where he demanded a white man take off his hat when he addressed my grandmother, but most of the family stories I heard revolved around my grandfather's drinking problem and absence from his children's lives.

When my father was about twelve, he went to an auto shop to meet his father, who worked there as a janitor. After arriving, my father said something that angered a white mechanic. The mechanic smacked him and shoved him to the ground.

Seething with anger, my father waited until his father appeared. The auto shop was small, so surely, he figured, his father must have seen what the white man did and would do something to stand up for his son.

My grandfather did appear, but he avoided looking at the white mechanic. He said nothing and showed no concern for his son, whose face still stung from the slap. Instead, he walked out of the shop, leading his son home.

"My father was a scared-ass nigger," my father said, the bitterness still dripping from his remark years later.

One of the reasons my father took a cab to see my mother was that he had decided early on that he wasn't going to live in fear of white people, like his father had. He was entitled to whatever white men had, including their most prized possessions—their women. But if I even suggested that he had taken a big risk in seeing my mother, he quickly waved away that characterization. "I didn't take risks," he told me. "I wanted to make sure I got a fair deal, whatever I did. During the forties and fifties, Black people didn't think of having the same things a white man had. Anything I did, I wanted to make sure it was equal. That's all that was."

But what made him think he could have the same things a white man had at a time when Black equality was absent in every sphere of American life? The nature of his merchant mariners job provided a crucial answer.

At the end of World War II, psychologists delved into the nature of racism and prejudice. Many were haunted by the Holocaust. They wanted to know how Nazi Germany was able to turn ordinary people into monsters. How do anti-Semitism and racial prejudice develop? Can people be cured of their racism, or is it an unalterable part of human nature? Those were some of the questions they asked.

One social scientist named Ira N. Brophy came up with an intriguing answer to some of those questions. He studied what happened when leaders of the Seafarers International Union, the largest merchant marine union, decided just before World War II to admit Black members.[6] The decision triggered protests and widespread resistance from white merchant mariners. Brophy said up to 68 percent of white seamen who had never sailed with Black men expressed racial prejudice.

Something unexpected took place, though, when those white mariners sailed with and worked alongside Black men.

The percentage of white sailors expressing racial prejudice steadily fell with each trip they took with Black merchant mariners, plummeting to 15 percent after four or more voyages.[7] It fell because of the nature of the job. Merchant mariners were isolated at sea for long periods of time, sharing rooms, bathrooms, mess halls—and especially danger from storms and war. The merchant marine suffered a higher casualty rate than any military branch in World War II—one in twenty-six died compared with one in thirty-four for the U.S. Marines.[8] The experience of shared danger meant that Black and white merchant mariners "could not afford the luxury of an anti-Negro prejudice at sea," Brophy wrote.[9]

Brophy's study of Black and white merchant mariners was later described as "the most powerful proof" of a concept known as "contact theory,"[10] a theory that originated with one of the twentieth century's most important psychologists, Gordon Allport. Allport said racial prejudice would decline if different racial groups had more contact with one another under certain conditions. Those conditions include both racial groups having contact in situations where they have common goals and equal status. (Slave masters shared physical proximity with slaves, but that didn't lead to more racial tolerance.)

My father was one of the first Black members of the Seafarers International Union—right around the time that Brophy conducted his study on the union. My father sailed in convoys across the North Atlantic during World War II, when white sailors were just learning to accept Black seamen as equals.

While Brophy's study focused on the transformative effects on white sailors, it didn't look at the impact on Black sailors like my father. Yet even without a study to prove it, it was just as transformative for my father.

A Black man couldn't have found a more integrated space in mid-twentieth-century America than the deck of a merchant marine ship. In 1940, the U.S. military was still eight years away from officially integrating following an executive order from President Truman. But white, Black, and brown sailors were already carrying out their own experiments with integration during the war.

My father pursued my mom with such boldness in part because that's the way he had been living for the most part for twenty years at sea—as a man who was treated as an equal.

My cousin Reese was no sociologist, but he had an illuminating response when I asked him why my father took such risks: "He didn't dock into a segregated world."

When I would rummage through his green duffel bag, I had glimpses of the freedom my father enjoyed while working overseas. I would often find pictures of him sitting at massive restaurant tables or in bunk rooms with smiling white sailors in places like Vietnam, Japan, and South Africa.

One day, while looking at those photos and hearing my father talk about his white friends, I thought, *Damn, he's had more contact and friendships with white people than I have, though he's the one who grew up in the Jim Crow era.*

That contact may have been the reason I never heard my father use racial slurs against white people or lump all white people into one category. I never even heard him speak in anger about my maternal grandfather, the man who assaulted him and tried to have him locked up for seeing his daughter.

"I never hated white people," he told me during one late-night conversation. "I hated the system."

But there was one storm that even my father, with all his resilience and experience, couldn't prepare for: my mother's mental illness.

The signs were subtle at first. After my parents moved in together, she got a job. That's when my father started noticing that things were off. He said my mom would turn the gas stove on and leave the apartment without turning the stove off or closing the door. She had a habit of disappearing without telling anyone, either for long bus rides that took her outside the city or on walks as long as ten miles.

My father would sit at home, worried that she might have been injured in an accident or attacked by someone.

"He would be in the house just moping and not eating," Twiggy said. "You couldn't talk to him."

One time when my mother disappeared, my father stayed by the phone. When it finally rang, he rushed to pick it up. "Shirley, where are you?" he said. "I missed you."

Twiggy, then a young man, watched the scene unfold. "He was damn near crying on the phone," Twiggy said. "I felt sorry for him. It was the first time I had heard him express feelings like that."

My mother seemed oblivious to what was happening to her.

She carried on as if nothing were wrong, and then she'd disappear from home again or lose another job.

My father soon discovered something even more shocking. My mother was using newspapers instead of sanitary napkins for her menstrual cycle. "She couldn't be left alone," he said. "She'd do crazy things."

The erratic behavior continued until it became too much, he told me. He decided to leave. But before he could, my mother became pregnant with me. They moved to New York City, to Brooklyn, where I was born. Then my mother's erratic behavior became dangerous.

For as long as I could recall, I'd had a dime-sized scar over my heart. I didn't know where it came from. When I was a kid, I'd ask my father about it, but he'd ignore my questions. After I met my mom, he started talking more about their time together. One night he reminisced about going dancing with her and listening to Tony Bennett together. Since he was in a jovial mood, I decided to ask: "Dad, where did I get this scar on my chest?"

His laugh trailed away, followed by a brief silence. "Well, it was—I don't like to talk about it," he finally said.

"I'm old enough to handle it," I pressed.

Not many months after I was born, he'd left me at home in the apartment with my mother so that he could run an errand. When he returned, he could hear me wailing behind the closed apartment door. He burst into the apartment, ran into the bedroom, and found me flailing on the bed, my arms and legs twitching. As he drew closer, he noticed the butt of a lit cigarette resting on my chest, right above my heart. My mother was beside me in bed and had apparently rubbed a smoldering cigarette on my chest to stop me from crying. He flicked the cigarette off my chest and picked me up to console me.

"I knew right away that I had to get you away from Shirley," he said.

I was too stunned to ask how my mother reacted. I didn't think to ask if she ignored me or if she knew what she had done. I felt no anger toward my mom, only sadness.

But though my mother was showing serious instability, my father didn't take me and leave, because my mom was pregnant with Pat. After she gave birth to my brother, they tried to stay together to raise their two sons. So they moved back to West Baltimore to get childcare help from my paternal grandmother, and my mom spent much of her time with my father's extended family.

My older relatives told me that my mother loved being our mom. She'd tickle our stomachs and rub her nose against ours. She'd hug us and rock us while serenading us with Doris Day's "Que Sera, Sera (Whatever Will Be, Will Be)" and Patsy Cline songs. They said she liked to play hide-and-seek with me, teasing me with "Where are you, John?" while I giggled. She even seemed to enjoy the mundane tasks of motherhood, like feeding us and changing our diapers.

"You and Pat would form a circle around her and hug her," my cousin Reese told me.

But soon my mother's behavior changed again. She became withdrawn and began mumbling to herself. People in my family started to notice. One day, my grandmother whispered to my father, "She has issues." Not long after, my family stopped leaving her alone with Pat and me.

"She got different, quiet. She started to drift," my brother Tony said. "She started to chain-smoke."

Although the causes of schizophrenia are unknown, pregnancy and birth complications have been associated with the onset of

the disease.[11] Research suggests that people who develop schizophrenia are more likely to have experienced complications before
and during their birth, if they had a family member with the illness. My father would learn later that my mother's mother had
been committed to a mental institution. My mom was only three
when it happened.

What happened next is unclear. I could never get a straight
answer. But less than a year after Patrick was born, my mom was
committed to a mental institution by her father.

There's an apocryphal family story that depicts my mother's
father storming into my family's house to take possession of her,
dragging her by the hair out of the house as she screamed for help.
I could never find anyone to corroborate that story. I don't know
if my father tried to stop my mother's institutionalization or how
my mother reacted. I can't imagine the pain of a young mother
being pulled away from her two babies. All I'm certain of is that
my mother's departure was sudden. The young, vibrant woman
who charmed my father's family stopped showing up.

"One day she was gone," my cousin Reese said. "One day became a week, and a week became a month, and then the rest is
history."

I could hear the pain in my father's voice when he talked about
my mom. "She tried, but she didn't have the capacity to do normal things," my father said. "She wanted to be accepted like a
normal person."

It wasn't racism that destroyed their relationship. It was mental
illness. It was one of the only topics more taboo than race in the
mid-1960s. There seemed to be no group or people more stigma-
tized and reviled than those who had a mental illness. Families
often sent those with mental illnesses away to places like Crownsville and refused to talk about them with outsiders.

"I didn't know what mental illness was all about," my father said. "I had to learn the hard way."

I had my own difficult learning curve. After meeting my mom, I continued to visit her and talk to her over the phone. I thought my presence would unlock something in her. But I didn't know what to say when I talked to her. And she would often forget a week later that I had ever been there.

I turned to letters as an alternative. I wrote long letters to her, telling her about my childhood, my dreams, and my hopes for our relationship.

I wouldn't receive a response for a long time. Then finally a letter would arrive, written in hasty, almost indecipherable cursive on paper torn from a notepad: "Dear John! I could use some money and to see you in person. I haven't heard from you in a long time. Could you send me a picture of yourself and Pat for Mother's Day? Love, Shirley."

I eventually gave up trying to summon the exuberant woman whom I first saw in that photograph.

Pat felt some of my frustration. She was a mother in name only. "She will never be able to tell me, 'I did this with you when you were a boy,' or what it was like when she took me to the first day of school or saw me first walk," he said.

Within a year of meeting my mom, I lost the desire to learn more about her or her family. Part of it was fear. Not only did each answer seem to make me more depressed, but I also wondered if I, too, would eventually suffer from what afflicted her. But I did my duty—I checked a box and met her, and I made sure to visit and send the coffee and Saint Jude medals she requested.

Meeting my mother didn't solve a problem; it created a new one. I had always been ashamed that my mother was white. Now I had a new shame: She also had schizophrenia.

I wanted to focus on the future, not the past. A new life outside Baltimore beckoned. I thought there was nothing more to learn about my mother or her family, and I was sure I would never meet the dynamic woman my father's family had known.

I was wrong.

CHAPTER 5

And Love Comes Gushing Down

John on Howard University campus

You just wait. You just wait," Twiggy said to me as he eased his sky-blue Pontiac Firebird through the rush-hour traffic toward our destination. "You mark my words."

I said nothing and stared out the window in glum silence as the unfamiliar streets passed by. I drummed my fingers against the armrest, sighing deeply to slow my shallow breathing. I felt like I was being driven to the gallows, and in a way I was. It was 1982, and I had just said goodbye to all I had ever known. I was leaving Baltimore for my freshman year of college in Washington, D.C.

"What if I don't make it?" I asked Twiggy. "What if I'm not smart enough?"

Twiggy chuckled and flipped on his blinker to turn left onto Georgia Avenue, one of the main thoroughfares in the nation's capital. He didn't bother to look at me. He just flashed a cocky smile. "If I can make it, you can make it," he said. "You're smarter than me. You read all them books, don't you?" And then he smiled again and repeated the same line I'd been hearing all morning: "You just wait. You just wait. These are going to be some of the best years of your life."

Twiggy pulled up a narrow side street, found a parking space, and turned the engine off. I stepped out of the car and stared wide-eyed at the sprawling college campus ahead of me. I had just arrived at the "Harvard of Black America." I was about to start my freshman year at Howard University, the most prestigious historically Black university in the nation.

My eyes settled on a massive four-story brick building with a clock tower. It was Founders Library, the centerpiece of the campus. Its clock tower soared so high that it could be seen throughout the nation's capital. Below the library was the Yard, a handsome, flat open space dotted with lush manicured lawns. Freshman students—some in J.Crew shorts and Dockers boat shoes, others in dashikis with dreadlocks—toted luggage and turntables to their dorms, pausing to greet one another with smiles and elaborate handshakes.

When I arrived that first year, Howard was surrounded by a grim inner-city backdrop: dilapidated brownstone homes, check-cashing stores, and fast-food chicken restaurants. But there was no better place for a young Black man to go if he wanted to run away from nagging questions about his white mother and his divided racial identity. Howard was the pre-eminent training ground for

Blackness, a place, as a popular T-shirt worn by students pro-claimed, where we were "Black by Popular Demand."

Howard was where the Black elite—the richest and most edu-cated Black families from around the globe—sent their children. My freshman class drew many of the nation's brightest Black stu-dents, along with others from Africa, the Middle East, and the Caribbean. One of my freshman classmates was an ambitious, photogenic student from Oakland, California. Her name was Kamala Harris, and she would go on to become the nation's first Black, South Asian, and female vice president.

As I grabbed my luggage to head to my dormitory, I looked at those impossibly poised Black students milling about. They looked like they had stepped out of the pages of a fashion maga-zine. And I thought of all the Black leaders who had graduated from Howard: civil rights leader Andrew Young; author Toni Morrison, who won a Nobel *and* a Pulitzer Prize; and Thurgood Marshall, the first Black member of the U.S. Supreme Court.

Then I asked myself, *What the hell am I doing here?*

The short answer to that question is that it was a fluke of re-gional geography.

When I was in high school, I couldn't envision myself in col-lege. I was convinced I'd end up working a blue-collar job or going into the military. But with the prodding of Aunt Sylvia and several of my high school teachers, I applied to Howard with the attitude of someone playing the lottery: *Maybe I'll get lucky.* But I knew I was grossly unprepared. No teachers guided me through the college application process. I took no college prep courses in high school. I took no prep courses for the SAT, the standardized test often required for college admissions. And when I did take the SAT, I scored an abysmal 830. I also applied to only one col-lege, Howard, and that was because it was a forty-five-minute drive from Baltimore and I had visited during a high school class trip.

That's not to say I was a bad student in high school. I was a voracious reader. All those years reading books in foster homes had paid off. I made the honor roll throughout high school and was voted "most likely to succeed." I even became an outstanding junior tennis player, playing number one on my team and earning a ranking as one of the state's top juniors by winning tournaments. I was the prototypical scholar-athlete.

Still, I was shocked when I received an acceptance letter.

Some of the best lessons I would learn, however, took place outside the classroom. About a week after moving into my dorm, I was playing a Jimi Hendrix album in my room. I heard a knock on my door while someone outside yelled, "Turn it up! Turn it up!"

I scooted off my bed, tossed a textbook aside, and opened the door. A clean-shaven student with thick black Clark Kent glasses, the build of a fullback, and an easy grin stood before me. He raised his hand and gave me a high five, then walked past me to the stereo before I could say anything.

"You like Hendrix?" he said.

"Yeah! You?"

"Hell yeah!"

His name was David. He came in and sat down at my desk, and we started talking about music. He was a business major, but his real love was music: Hendrix, Sly Stone, and jazz fusion groups like Weather Report. I sat on my bed and watched him sort through the albums stacked on my desk.

"Where you from?" I asked him.

"Denver. You?"

"Bmore."

"Ah, Baltimore," he said, flashing another big smile. "Charm City."

"They got Black people in Denver?" I asked, half in jest. "I've never been in Denver. What's it like?"

He shot up from the desk chair he had commandeered. "I'll be back."

He left the room and returned with a book, which he handed to me. "Check it out," he said.

My jaw dropped as I flipped through the pages of his high school yearbook.

What kind of place? I thought. I looked up from the book and stared at David.

"This is where you went to school? With all these white people?"

"Yeah," he said, shrugging as he opened the album sleeve to my Hendrix *Band of Gypsys* album cover. "You ever listen to 'Machine Gun'? Now, that's the jam."

I was more interested in what I was seeing than hearing. As I scanned David's yearbook, I saw a grand high school that looked like a college campus, and I saw something else: page after page of Black students sharing classrooms with white students. On some of those pages, I saw David, with the same disarming grin, posing with white football teammates or joking with white students in a school club.

"Gotta go," David said, standing up. "You gotta let me play you some Weather Report."

I said goodbye to David and walked him to the door. But something about his yearbook kept bugging me. My unease grew as I had the same experience with other classmates. We developed a ritual of exchanging yearbooks when talking about where we came from, and I kept bumping into the same optics: my classmates posing comfortably with white students in magnificent high schools that made my high school in Baltimore look like a rural one-room schoolhouse. The students I met from southern states like Alabama and North Carolina surprised me more. The student bodies in those yearbooks were even more racially mixed than David's.

Those yearbooks had as much impact on me as any book I cracked open in a classroom. I knew on an intellectual level that I had attended only racially segregated Black public schools. It didn't hit me emotionally, though, until I met other students like David. Because I grew up in the Northeast, I thought I lived in a more racially accepting environment than Black students in the South and elsewhere in the country. I had an image of the South and other parts of the country as backward regions where the races stayed apart. I thought I was living in the racially enlightened North. So I was shocked to learn that Black students in places like Colorado and Alabama had more exposure to whites than I did.

That exposure gave them something I didn't have—confidence. In and out of the classrooms, they carried themselves with such self-assurance. They bantered with our teachers as if they were intellectual equals, and they gave crisp answers during classroom discussions. Many had already taken some of the college classes we attended, and they glided through lessons that I struggled with.

What was most impressive was what I learned in the late-night dorm conversations I had with friends like David. They didn't talk about white people like I did—no insecurity or anger. White people were their high school buddies, not this malevolent group I had imagined. And they weren't intimidated by white people like I had always been.

I still carried the psychic scars from Baltimore. I felt like an impostor at Howard. I was self-conscious about my West Baltimore accent and potentially mangling subject-verb agreements in classroom discussions. So I sat in the back of class, saying nothing unless called on.

When one of my West Baltimore buddies called me one day and asked what Howard was like, I told him I had never been around such polished Black people who enunciated every syllable and never mangled subject-verb agreements. "Man, this is the first time I've been around Black people who can talk," I said.

Since I didn't feel like I belonged, I acted like I didn't. Because I was homesick, I stopped going to classes and studying. I missed my friends in West Baltimore. By the end of my freshman year, I had been put on academic probation. One more bad semester, and I would go home in disgrace.

I was facing these challenges at the same time my nephew Mike was going through his. We had both entered a new world—me at Howard, he at my brother Twiggy's suburban home. He chose to go back to what was familiar. I initially made the same choice, because I was doing everything I could to flunk out and return to Baltimore.

So what changed for me? A long walk home one night in the fall of my sophomore year. I had a big test coming up in my science class. If I didn't get a good grade, I would flunk out. My panic increased as the date of the test approached. One night, I decided to take a walk back from the main campus to my dormitory to clear my head. I slung a bag holding my tennis racket and a book over my shoulder and started on my mile-long journey.

If I fail, Aunt Sylvia is going to be so hurt, I thought as I walked past a Church's Chicken shop on Georgia Avenue, the same road that Twiggy had used a year earlier to bring me to Howard.

I thought about my father, the look of disgust I would see on his face, and the disapproving words I'd heard before: "John, you don't know shit about shit."

I walked downhill on a street lined with disheveled row houses, leaves crunching under my scruffy white Reebok tennis shoes. It was late and cold. I flipped the collar of my navy peacoat up over my ears and tried to think of what I could do well. *I play tennis well,* I thought.

The discipline imposed by tennis had become a part of my makeup. I spent hours on the court, practicing drills until I was exhausted. It took focus and patience. I would practice one stroke, like a forehand crosscourt shot, for thirty minutes straight until I got it right.

On my walk back to my dorm, I stopped and nodded. I would approach school like tennis. I told myself that I would study as hard as I could, like I trained on the tennis court. If I could focus two hours in practice, I could apply the same discipline to the classroom. And if I did flunk out, at least I would be able to say I tried my best.

I picked up the pace back to my dorm. When I got to my room, I didn't put on music or go to sleep. I sat at my desk and cracked open a book.

I earned an A on the science test and was one of only three students to pass it in my class. My grades picked up. Instead of flunking out, I ended up paying for college through a series of academic scholarships awarded to students with a high grade point average.

That change, though, couldn't have been sustained without something else: the help I received from friends like David. As I formed friendships with Black students who came from more affluent backgrounds, they tutored me when I ran into difficult subjects, gave me books to read, and exposed me to new music and new ways of thinking. They told me in word and deed something I needed to know: *You belong here.*

The most important person who did this for me was my college girlfriend. Her name was Susan, and she was the daughter of a child psychiatrist and a school principal who lived in Baldwin Hills, California, a posh predominantly Black suburb in Los Angeles. She attended a prestigious public high school in Beverly Hills that drew the children of celebrities. And she spent a year at Stanford University before enrolling at Howard.

Susan was a slim woman with hazel eyes and cherub cheeks dotted with freckles. I met her in the college cafeteria, where we usually sat near each other. I remember her casually mentioning during a study session that her family's maid was like part of the family.

My jaw dropped again.

"You have a *maid*?" I asked.

She looked at me with a shrug and smile that said "And?"

I was even more impressed when I visited her home one summer break. It sat on top of a hill overlooking Los Angeles, complete with a swimming pool out back and a Jacuzzi in her parents' bedroom. Her parents were warm, gracious people who chatted with me about my future over dinner. I stammered through the conversation, wondering if I was holding my fork correctly and feeling humiliated when Susan took me aside after I called her father "Mr. James" during dinner.

"Please call him Dr. James," Susan whispered. "He's a doctor, not a mister."

I didn't talk much about my mother to Susan. I told her she was white, but not much else. I wasn't prepared to explain my upbringing to anyone, because I didn't know how to explain it to myself. I didn't want to think about my past. I wanted to focus on the future. And Susan helped convince me that I had one. One night while we were studying and talking, she dropped her pen onto her paper and said, "John, you're just as smart as any of the students I met at Stanford."

I wouldn't have made it without friends like Susan and David. They and others like them at Howard would go on to become big-city mayors, surgeons, Hollywood actors, and business executives. One could say that their success was due to their parents' sacrifices and their own motivation. They decided to work hard and made no excuses.

But then I think about those yearbook photos, and the reason for those people's success is more complicated. It wasn't just because of their hard work. It was also a result of a golden period of racial progress in the United States that has been erased from public memory.

Mention school integration, and it evokes images of traumatized Black schoolchildren in the 1960s and '70s staring out of yellow-school-bus windows while angry white parents march outside with signs like "No Forced Busing!" The movement to integrate the nation's public schools is widely portrayed as a failed social experiment.

Sure, the Supreme Court desegregated public schools in its landmark *Brown v. Board of Education* decision in 1954. But anyone who follows history knows that the decision sparked massive resistance. White parents in the South withdrew their kids from schools that started admitting Black students and either moved to suburban whiter schools or created private white-only schools for their children,[1] often billing these schools as Christian academies. Northern white parents took a savvier approach. They often used

race-neutral terms like *busing* to disguise their opposition to sending their kids to schools with Black students.[2]

But beginning in the mid-1960s, the courts and the U.S. Congress enforced the *Brown* decision. They threatened to withhold
federal funds from public schools that didn't desegregate.[3] They
bused white and non-white students to other schools to create
more racially mixed schools. This process accelerated in the 1970s
and '80s despite the disapproval of the increasingly conservative
Supreme Court. And something astonishing happened: The test-
score gap between Black and white children was dramatically re-
duced, without compromising the academic performance of
white students.[4] Many white students who attended schools with
Black and brown students later said that what they experienced
enriched their lives beyond academics, making them more empa-
thetic and aware of issues they would have never thought of in a
segregated setting.[5]

During a golden fifteen-year period that peaked in 1988, the
United States saw "the greatest racial convergence of achievement
gaps [and] educational attainment," said Rucker C. Johnson, a
professor of public policy at the University of California, Berkeley, who specializes in the economics of education.[6]

American public schools have since resegregated to 1968 levels,
even as the nation grows more diverse.[7] A conservative Supreme
Court has made it virtually impossible to use race to increase diversity at public schools,[8] and many affluent white parents prefer
to send their kids to private schools, which tend to be more racially homogenous.

My Howard classmates like David were the beneficiaries of this
golden period. They had walked through a door that was already
closing by the time we got to Howard. They attended well-

funded integrated schools in the 1970s, while I attended a racially segregated school in the part of the country that resisted integration more than any other: the Northeast.[9] I didn't have the exposure, academically or culturally, that they did. No wonder I felt so insecure.

I saw this golden period embodied in all those self-assured students I met at Howard. But the successful effort to integrate white and Black students has been suppressed by what author and journalist Nikole Hannah-Jones called "one of the most successful propaganda campaigns of the last half century."[10]

"Our one real effort to bring the promises of Brown to fruition withered amid the belief that we had tried really hard and failed," she wrote in an essay. "But to say busing—or really, mandated desegregation—failed is a lie. . . . Busing did not fail. We did."[11]

There are those who might argue that the success of historically Black colleges like Howard shows that integration is overrated. After all, they produced excellent college graduates in a racial setting that was primarily Black. But schools like Howard were never meant to be the norm. They were founded during the Jim Crow era because Black students were denied admittance to white schools. And as prestigious as Howard is, it and other Black colleges like it have never gotten close to having the type of endowment and resources that elite white colleges have.

I loved my time at Howard, and I think there's a place for historically Black colleges. But I'm also reminded of something Hannah-Jones said during an interview with National Public Radio about school integration: "There's never been a moment in the history of this country where Black people who have been isolated from white people have gotten the same resources."[12]

. . .

David's knock on my dormitory door that first week at Howard forced me to rethink my past. Another knock on my door a year later changed my plans for the future.

I was in my sophomore year at Howard when I heard a gentle tapping on my dorm door one late afternoon. I opened it to see a thin young Black man with brushed-back wavy hair, caramel skin, and high cheekbones. His eyes darted about in confusion when he saw me.

"I think I have the wrong room," he said.

"That's all right," I said as I started to close the door.

He pointed at me. "Wait a minute," he said. "I've seen you before, haven't I?"

I studied his face. Yeah, I had seen him, too, in the student cafeteria. He sat near where I usually ate with Susan.

"Yeah, my name is John," I said, still standing in the doorway.

"Ah, my name is Darren," he said.

We shook hands.

He remained standing in my doorway, nodding silently as if trying to figure out what to say next.

I moved to close the door. "Okay," I said. "I'll catch up with you later."

He held up his right hand to stop me. "Ah, we have a Bible talk every Wednesday night downstairs called 'Soul Talk.' Would you be interested in joining us?"

I stifled an impulse to laugh out loud. I had just escaped from church prison with Aunt Sylvia. The last thing I wanted to do in college was go back to spending long hours in church. Besides, I thought the Bible was riddled with contradictions and scientific impossibilities. Still, that afternoon I was bored, and I loved to argue—about religion, politics, anything—so I said, "I don't know about going to any Bible talk, but if you want to come in and talk about the Bible, I'm okay with that."

Darren's eyes brightened. He smiled and walked in, carrying a burgundy leather Thompson Chain-Reference Bible.

And that's how it started: Tuesdays with Darren. I refused to go to Soul Talk, but I accepted his proposal to come by my dorm room every Tuesday night to study the Bible.

It didn't matter how much ice or snow covered the ground; I'd peek out my window just before 7 P.M. every Tuesday, and I'd see Darren bouncing up to the dormitory entrance in his scruffy white leather tennis shoes and grungy sweater to talk to me. I couldn't understand it. *What's his angle?* I wondered. *Why is this so important to him?*

I experienced no bolt of lightning while reading the Bible with Darren. He never convinced me that the Bible was infallible or that an Adam and Eve once traipsed through a Garden of Eden. Darren was an engineering major, a soft-spoken and shy young man who sometimes stammered when I hit him with a barrage of questions. But he had a photographic recall of Scripture, and he introduced me to the New International Version of the Bible. For the first time, I could understand what I was reading. I was drawn to the stories in the New Testament, not specific doctrines.

Like many other Black people, I had an ambivalent perception of Jesus because of how he's traditionally been portrayed in religion and popular culture. He was the white guy with blond hair and blue eyes whose portrait loomed above the pulpit of my childhood church. And the New Testament was that part of the Bible that white slave masters invoked when they quoted scriptures like Colossians 3:22: "Slaves, obey your earthly masters in

everything." I had never had much use for that Jesus or the book.
I was more drawn to Eastern sages like Gautama Buddha or Lao-
tzu.

The Jesus that Darren guided me to wasn't what I expected. At
times, he sounded like a Zen master with his pithy, paradoxical
sayings: "Whoever finds his life will lose it, and whoever loses his
life for my sake will find it."[13] In other passages, he sounded like
an action hero, denouncing hypocritical religious leaders and
chasing the money changers out of Jerusalem's temple with a
whip he fashioned from cords.

What spoke deeper to me, though, were the stories of Jesus
obliterating any divisions—ethnic, gender, class—that stood between people. He welcomed a Zealot and a tax collector into his
inner circle. (Imagine a leader who convinces a Ku Klux Klan
member and a Nation of Islam member to call each other brother.)
And the first Christian church was a radically egalitarian place
where slaves and women became leaders and where people shared
wealth along with power.

One scripture that Darren steered me to stuck: "There is neither Jew nor Greek, slave nor free, male nor female, for you are all
one in Christ Jesus."[14]

I had struggled with my identity because of race. Now here
was a way to define myself beyond the whims of white or Black
people.

I did something I had never thought I'd do again. I tagged
along to Darren's church on Sunday. It was a white evangelical
church whose leaders made interracial solidarity a primary mission of their church. All the scriptures that he shared with me
couldn't compare to what I saw: Black, white, and brown people
worshipping together. They greeted one another with bear hugs
and laughter and called one another brother and sister. They hung

out outside church for pizza and informal Bible talks and even dated one another.

This snapshot of interracial unity in the pews—not what I read in the Bible about Jesus walking on water—was the real miracle to me.

It was the mid-1980s, and churches were routinely segregated. There were no national movements for racial reconciliation or rallies by groups like Promise Keepers, a non-profit evangelical men's group that pushed its white members to build bridges with non-white Christians. What the Reverend Martin Luther King, Jr., said in a 1960 interview still applied: "Eleven o'clock on Sunday morning is one of the most segregated hours, if not the most segregated hour, in Christian America."[15]

Darren pressed me to get baptized, but I preferred to keep my appreciation of faith on an intellectual level. The semester ended, and I moved to Chicago for the summer after being awarded an internship at the *Chicago Tribune*. I was thinking of becoming a journalist. My family always had newspapers and magazines scattered around the house. I knew the power of stories from reading so much in foster homes. Maybe, I thought, I could tell stories in newspapers to help people.

I enjoyed my time at Darren's church so much that I decided to attend a Bible study in suburban Chicago. The Bible-study group was part of the same interracial-church movement Darren belonged to.

I drove into a picturesque, leafy suburban neighborhood filled with brownstone apartments. I grabbed a Bible that I had just purchased, got out of the car, and reached into my pocket to make sure I still had the address written on a slip of paper. A short walk took me to an apartment with large bay windows out front and potted flowers by the door. As I headed up the steps, I peeked through the open windows and saw a handful of young people sitting on couches in the living room, Bibles in their laps, smiling and chatting.

My heart sank. My right hand hovered over the doorbell, but I dropped it with a sigh. *Damn,* I thought as I turned around. *Nothing but white people.*

I didn't want to ring the doorbell, because I didn't want to be the dreaded Only Black Guy in the Room. I had been in integrated church settings before, but now I was going to be alone in the house with a group of white strangers.

I started walking down the steps, away from the apartment, then stopped. *Don't chicken out,* I told myself. *If you don't like them, you don't have to come back.*

I turned around, walked up the steps, took a deep breath, and knocked on the door.

A young white man with a thick blond mustache swung open the door with a smile. "Welcome, brother," he said as he gestured toward the living room. "Come on in. What's your name?"

I ended up having one of the best summers of my life. I met Jim Gallagher, a jovial white Irish editor at the *Chicago Tribune,* who taught me that I could use my background growing up in West Baltimore to write about subjects other reporters would miss. He invited me to his home to have dinner with his family and took me to lunch, always ending the conversation with the same type of advice: "You are much better than you know. You can write about experiences that all these other reporters wouldn't know anything about." I took Jim's advice that summer and wrote an article about almost flunking out at Howard that won the college equivalent of the Pulitzer Prize.

But the most dramatic change came in my personal life. I became close friends with two young men in that study, including the one who had answered the door. His name was Paul, and he was an illustrator who exuded a sense of peace and acceptance that made me feel instantly comfortable. The other friend was Andy, a tall, thin man with a huge Adam's apple who was a magician. I spent many nights in that apartment that summer, long after Bible study ended, talking with Paul and Andy about the things all young men think about at that age: our dreams for the future, our girlfriends, and our personal struggles. On Sundays, I'd see them in church. And now I was the one giving bro hugs to white people in church.

Paul and Andy were white evangelical Christians. They were the first people I formed close interracial relationships with, and they were the ones who first showed me that faith could be stronger than someone's racial prejudice.

I kept meeting other white Christians who inspired me.

I couldn't find a place to stay that summer, so I ended up renting a room in a former convent in suburban Chicago. The convent was the home base for a white missionary couple, Frank and Aimee. I spent many hours with Frank in particular, talking about race and my questions about the Bible and hearing stories of his travels. He gave me books to read. But what I remember most is how he and his fellow missionaries sang.

A group of them would file into the house about once a week to eat and pray together. Afterward, they would retire to a study and sing hymns. It wasn't the Black gospel music I grew up with, but as I lay on my bed in my cramped room, I could hear their joyous voices echo through the hallways of the old convent.

When I left to return to Howard, Frank gave me a hug, then said, "John, I envy your future."

I returned to Howard for my junior year and met up with

Darren. He pressed again for a decision on baptism. I still wasn't ready. Then something odd happened. I started having strangers approach me on campus, asking me when I was going to give my life to Christ. None of them knew Darren or were affiliated with his church. They were just random people who decided they had to talk to me about giving my life to Christ. *Do I look that sinful?* I thought as yet another person on campus asked me about my relationship with Christ.

The tension started to build within me. I felt a stirring, a feeling that I had to make a decision about my faith. There were too many coincidences piling up: Darren knocking on the door, my finding a place to stay in Chicago run by missionaries, and the strangers approaching me. It all came to a head when I returned to Baltimore for Christmas break.

It was Christmas Eve, and I was walking toward a subway station in West Baltimore. The sidewalk was packed with pedestrians hustling home with hefty shopping bags. Donny Hathaway's soulful voice belted out "This Christmas" from a passing car radio. The sun was setting, casting violet streaks across the horizon, and people nodded and smiled at one another as they passed on the street.

I should have been in the holiday spirit, but I was preoccupied. I'd had a troubling phone conversation with a high school buddy named David the night before. For some reason David brought up Christianity, a subject we never talked about. "No blond, blue-eyed Christ for me," he said. "My oppressor doesn't get to set himself as my God. I can't be the blind believer who stops thinking or questioning. Worse is the arrogance that tells some people that they and Gawwd are so close that they're on his pay-roll and that makes their actions justified. Too much evil is done in the name of religion."

I thought of Darren and all the other Christians I'd recently met. I took a half-hearted stab at saying that not all Christians were like that. We ended the conversation after talking about something else, and I hung up the phone, shaking my head in disgust at myself. I felt like a hypocrite, defending Christians without being one myself.

David has an excuse—he hasn't had the experiences I've had, I thought. What was mine? What was holding me back? Before I went to bed that night, I made a vow: *The next time someone talks to me about Jesus, I'm going to make a decision.*

As I rushed toward the subway the next day, I was concerned with something else. Someone was following me. I glanced over my right shoulder and spotted a young Black man across the street weaving in and out of the sidewalk traffic with his eyes on me.

As I rounded a corner to head to the subway entrance, I heard the young man shout, "Hey, friend!"

I stopped, turned, and saw him standing across the street. He was a big, bulky guy with a short, matted Afro and a chipped front tooth, and he wore dusty construction boots. He jogged toward me, pausing to allow traffic to pass by. I squinted at him, trying to figure out where I had seen him before.

Is he someone I know from high school? I wondered. *Why can't I remember him?*

Then my body tensed. I started looking to my left and my right. *Maybe this is a setup, a robbery?* I thought.

I didn't keep walking, though, because his smile held me in place. It was so warm, like we had known each other all our lives.

He reached me and stopped to catch his breath. Then his smile disappeared, and he looked at me with utmost seriousness. "Don't you know that there are so many things in this world that are taking you away from Jesus Christ?" he said.

I dropped my hands to my sides and lowered my head. I immediately recalled my resolution the night before: *The next time someone talks to me about Jesus, I'm going to make a decision.*

A white guy with glasses and shaggy brown hair jogged up to us and stood next to the Black man. He had a Bible in his hand, just like the guy who had stopped me.

"What do I have to do?" I said in a tone that was more resigned than joyful. "What do I have to do?"

He smiled. We talked. I told them about my conversation the night before and the silent vow I'd made.

Raising his eyebrows, he turned to his white companion, who smiled for the first time.

"Praise God!" the Black man said.

We were clogging traffic on a packed street corner, with people streaming by, some stealing curious glances at our impromptu public meeting.

"Listen," I said. "I don't know if I can do this. I can't be perfect."

The Black man looked at his white friend again. Then he opened a small leather-bound Bible and pointed at a highlighted passage.

"I haven't had a perfect day yet, and I never will," he said. "But I'm confident of this." And then he read Philippians 1:6: "Being confident of this, that he who began a good work in you will carry it on to completion until the day of Christ Jesus."

He must be related to Darren, I thought absentmindedly as he read. *He has a scripture for every question.*

"So what am I supposed to do?" I said.

"It's not complicated," he said. He opened his Bible to another passage: "If you confess with your mouth, 'Jesus is Lord,' and believe in your heart that God raised him from the dead, you will be saved."[16]

I thought about what he'd said. The swirling street scene went silent. Nothing else mattered. This was the most important moment of my life.

He extended his hands to me, palms up. His friend did the same.

"Let's pray," he said.

I reached out and took both men's hands—white, black, and brown hands joined on a chilly street corner.

I said the prayer: "Dear Lord Jesus, I know that I am a sinner, and I ask for your forgiveness. I believe you died for my sins and rose from the dead. I turn from my sins and invite you to come into my heart and life. I want to trust and follow you as my Lord and Savior."

I opened my eyes to see the Black man smiling. He hugged me. So did his friend.

"My name is Albert," the Black man said before introducing me to his friend, whose name I promptly forgot. He reached into his pocket and gave me a pamphlet. It was a pocket-sized copy of the gospel of John. When I opened it, I could see his name written inside along with his phone number.

"Take this home and read it," he said. "If you have any questions, call me."

I nodded again. He gave me the same smile and a bear hug and then walked away. The noise of the Christmas bustle returned. I resumed walking toward the subway. I turned around once more to say thanks. But he and his friend had vanished, swallowed by the sidewalk traffic.

I caught the subway home to my father's house, where an exasperated Pat waited for me by the front door.

"Where you been?" he said. "I've been waiting for you."

I said nothing and walked by him. I went to my old bedroom, the one I hardly ever used anymore now that I was in college. I closed the door, flopped onto the bed, and opened the pamphlet Albert had given me. I had never read one of the Gospels in its entirety, until now.

I started reading, sinking into the story, losing track of time. I stopped at John 12:32: "I, when I am lifted up from the earth, will draw all men to myself." I knew in that moment that I was one of countless people who were being drawn to Jesus. The creator of the universe wanted me enough to chase me down on a street corner. How could I say no?

I closed the pamphlet after I got to the end. I sat up on the bed, still digesting the events of the day. Suddenly I felt a curious sensation under my shirt. Alarmed, I lifted it to see what was wrong.

Did I hurt myself? I wondered.

My chest looked normal. I lowered my shirt, but I still felt a burning sensation in my chest. It felt like a flame burning above my heart, right above the spot where my mother had rubbed a cigarette butt on me.

At the end of the gospel of Luke, there's a passage about Jesus appearing after his resurrection to two disciples on the road to Emmaus. After Jesus left them, one of the disciples turned to the other and said, "Were not our hearts burning within us while he talked with us on the road and opened the Scriptures to us?"[17]

That passage took on a new meaning when I read it again. That's how I felt that night reading the gospel of John: My heart caught fire.

I returned to Howard and shared the news with Darren. He

smiled like a father seeing his child graduate. And he promptly arranged for my baptism. On the Sunday following my baptism, he asked me if I could go downstairs to the church meeting hall. When I entered, I saw a group of church members milling about. Puzzled, I watched them silently assemble like a flash mob and form a circle around me. They were white, Black, and Asian, both old and young.

They grasped hands and looked at me with beaming smiles, then started to sing:

John, we love you, we love you, we love you.
And love comes gushing down.
Ask anyone; give a little knock and the door will open.
And love comes gushing down.

I lowered my head in embarrassment, my face turning bright red.

After they finished, they all walked forward and wrapped their arms around me. I could only stand there in embarrassed silence.

Their embrace brought to mind another scripture I'd studied with Darren in my dorm room. It was Ephesians 3:20: "Now to him who is able to do immeasurably more than all we ask or imagine, according to his power that is at work within us . . ."

That scripture offered me a beautiful promise from God: "As much as you imagine happiness, I can offer you something so much better."

I'd never imagined that I would one day hug white people in a church and call them brother and sister. Now I was living that scripture.

. . .

I had a conversion experience in the classroom as well. After almost flunking out my sophomore year, I took flight as a student, making straight A's my last three semesters, save for one B. I couldn't believe it. I was going to graduate from Howard.

On a radiant spring day, I walked again into the Yard. This time I knew I belonged. I wore graduation robes and a tassel that declared I was graduating with honors, summa cum laude.

Camille Cosby, Bill Cosby's wife, was our commencement speaker. I don't remember what she said. I was thinking of one person as I sat in a folding chair in the Yard, scanning the crowd for her. After Cosby finished, I joined my classmates, including Susan and David, as we threw our mortarboards and tassels into the air. I started searching the crowd for the person who was on my mind: Aunt Sylvia.

I spotted her at the edge of the crowd, a tiny figure in a floral dress. Pat had been standing next to her but left her side to search for me. She was looking at me with the same contented smile she flashed whenever I made her proud. I walked toward her, weaving through celebrating students, keeping my eyes on her the whole time. When I got to her, I reached down and hugged her tight. When I finally pulled away, she took off her glasses and wiped happy tears away.

She handed me an envelope. When I returned to my dorm that night to finish packing, I sat down in my now-bare room and opened the envelope. A graduation card with a poem tumbled out. It read,

> *Lord, let me be your follower.*
> *Let me be your friend.*
> *Let me hear your voice and heed your call.*
> *Let me know the special plans you have for me. . . .*

I looked at the other side of the card and saw Aunt Sylvia's florid cursive writing filling the page. Her note read, "Dear John. My! How my heart rejoiced as I watched you process in the graduation ceremonies. My mind went back to when I first enrolled you in Head Start. Then I watched you as you made your accomplishments in Walbrook and then at Howard University. Love, Aunt Sylvia."

My father didn't attend my graduation, but I didn't dwell on it. He scoffed at my love of school. He just didn't get the world of books and academics. But Twiggy was right: These were some of the best years of my life.

I had met my mother, joined an interracial church, and made white friends. Soon I would land my first job as a newspaper reporter. If you had asked me then if I had accepted my mother and her family, I would have said, "Of course I have," and thrown a bunch of scriptures at you to prove my case.

But I would soon discover that there were bitter regions in my heart that not even the flame of God had extinguished.

CHAPTER 6

An Unexpected Meeting

Aunt Mary

first spotted her on a rainy summer day, standing on the front porch of a yellow antebellum-style house. She had a thin, angular face and a slim frame that looked familiar. When Pat and I walked toward the house, our gazes met hers. She stood waiting for us with a tight smile.

Pat and I were in our mid-twenties and had moved away from Baltimore after graduating from college. We had returned to Baltimore that day to visit our mother because she had been released from Crownsville and was now living in a group home for those who were being treated for mental illness. The home was run by a woman we simply knew as Miss Jones, a middle-aged Jamaican with a Jheri curl.

We had also returned home because Miss Jones had called me several weeks earlier to tell me that someone wanted to meet Pat and me. As Pat and I walked up her front steps, Miss Jones opened her screen door and came out to the porch to stand next to the thin white woman.

"John, Pat," Miss Jones said, gesturing toward the woman, who was staring intently at me, "this is your mother's sister. This is your Aunt Mary."

Patrick smiled and shook her hand as they exchanged greetings. Aunt Mary turned to me and extended her hand.

I just nodded as her hand hung in the air.

I had attended an interracial church. I had white friends. And I could quote copious scriptures on the need to forgive one's enemies and how God sees no color because we are "all one in Christ Jesus."[1] But when it came to meeting my mother's sister, the spirit may have been willing but the flesh was weak.

The woman who stood before me was someone I had never wanted to meet. My perception of her had been shaped by what my father and other family members had told me: *She's a racist; she doesn't like Black people. She's not like your mom.*

Her absence during my childhood validated those accusations. I knew from my father that she didn't have a mental illness. Her affliction was racism, I concluded. That was why I had never heard from her.

And now here she was, standing before me with an outstretched hand. I didn't want to take it. But then I thought of one of Aunt Sylvia's pithy sayings: *God don't like ugly.*

So I reached out and gave her a limp handshake.

Her shoulders relaxed. We all stood there looking at one another.

"Let's go inside," Miss Jones said.

We sat at the dining room table, where Miss Jones left us alone. There was awkward silence. Then she made small talk: Where had we gone to college? What did we do for a living? Where did we live?

The meeting was a blur. In some ways, I reacted to her like I did when I first met my mother. I got tunnel vision. I just kept looking at Aunt Mary, tuning everything else out.

She asked Pat where he had gone to school.

"I went to Bowie State," he said.

As Pat talked, I studied her body language. She was still, reserved, someone who seemed more comfortable listening than talking. She wasn't what I'd expected. I'd been expecting a loud, mean, blustery racist.

The meeting itself had come as a surprise. When I called Pat about a week earlier at his home in Charlotte, North Carolina, to discuss the invitation, I told him that I didn't want to meet our aunt.

"What's the use?" I said. "She didn't care to meet us when we really needed her."

The time for family reunions had passed, Pat said. It was too late to forge new bonds. "I'm happy and content just knowing Mom."

Still, I agreed to the meeting. I was curious. What did she want? What did she look like? Maybe she could tell me more about my mother's family.

I also agreed because I wanted something else from her: an apology for her racism.

It became clear after about twenty minutes of small talk that no apology or explanation would be forthcoming.

The frown I'd greeted her with returned to my face. I started to slide my chair away from the table, ready to stand up and go.

"I thought I might show you something," she said, reaching into the shopping bag she had with her. She pulled out several Ziploc bags, opened them, and spread the contents on the table. They were photographs.

I scooted my chair closer to the table to get a better look.

"This is your family," she said, looking at me. "We're the descendants of Irish immigrants. . . ."

It was like watching another home movie, but this time it was my white family. I studied the faces of my Irish relatives in these old sepia-toned photographs. They were portraits and quick snapshots of white people. Some are posing stiffly in formal portraits from the early twentieth century. Some are sitting on park benches or porches, chatting merrily away. Others are mugging for the camera.

"And this is your mother," she said.

I reached out and held up the miniature photograph, showing it to Pat. In the photo, my mom is no more than five, a little blond girl in her white communion dress, holding a bouquet of white flowers while squinting in the sunlight. A cross dangles from her neck as she smiles shyly at the camera.

I handed the photo to Pat and looked away.

"These are some of your aunts and uncles. . . ."

I resumed looking at all the photographs of my extended white family. I could see traces of my mother: the same brows, cheekbones, chin, and thick prematurely gray hair. I studied the photos, looking for traces of myself. *And where are they now?* I wondered. *What would they think of having Black relatives?*

I was smiling now. So was Pat. He pulled his chair closer to the table. We were finally seeing another side of our family tree. I was watching pieces of a family puzzle come together.

"Hey, Pat, check this out," I said, showing him a picture of our maternal grandmother standing in a nurse's uniform from what seemed like the 1940s. She was a lanky woman who stood five feet ten. I was average size at that point, but Pat had shot up from a skinny kid called "Bones" to a six-foot-two, two-hundred-pound young man.

"That's where you get your height from," I said.

Pat grinned as he took the photograph from me.

"And this," Aunt Mary said as she reached into another Zip-loc bag and slid a photograph across the table, "is your grand-father."

Our smiles evaporated. A chill swept through my body. The hairs on my forearms stood on end. I glanced at Pat, who returned my look with the same wide-eyed expression.

A young white man with thick coal-black hair brushed back from his face stared directly at the camera in a portrait photo that looked like it was taken in the 1930s. He had a square jaw and dark, brooding eyes that exuded no warmth. This was the man who had called my father a n*****. This was the man who had called the police on my father when he tried to visit my mother. This was the man who had died not long after Pat and I were born, never bothering to meet us because we were Black.

This was the man who had appeared in our bedroom years before, when we were children, the ghostly visitor who took my birthday cards.

This was our grandfather.

I said nothing to Aunt Mary. Neither did Pat. The meeting was already tense enough. A question like "Hey, did you know that your dead father paid us a visit years ago?" would have been a conversation stopper.

The meeting was so emotionally draining that Pat and I repressed parts of it for years. I forgot that our mother had been there at the house during our meeting with Aunt Mary; Pat forgot that it had happened at all.

By this time, I didn't want to learn more about my mother's family. I had no interest in talking to Aunt Mary again or even hearing from other members of my mother's family. Every time I learned something new about them, it was bad. I'd had enough disappointment in my life. I returned to my job as a newspaper reporter in Los Angeles, Pat to his job as a warehouse manager in Charlotte, North Carolina. I wanted to look to the future.

My mother's sister refused to let that happen. She did what I tried to do when I first met my mom. She tried to establish a relationship through letters. She mailed me a steady stream of letters containing more family photos and questions about my upbringing. She called and we talked.

I listened because I harbored the same fear that many in a similar situation have experienced. I wondered if I would be touched by the same illness my mother had.

I knew racism could destroy people's lives. Mental illness could do the same. In fact, mental illness may be worse because many of its victims either don't know what is happening to them or are too ashamed to talk openly about it.

I learned that mental illness had virtually destroyed my mother's family. My mother's sister said that my maternal grandmother, Anne Gladys Jones, began exhibiting signs of mental illness when my mom was as young as three. She flushed money down the toilet, thinking it was covered in germs, and sometimes forgot the names of her two daughters. My grandfather eventually decided to commit her when her behavior proved too erratic.

My grandfather became a single parent. He was a poor, working-class man trying to raise two girls alone on what little money he made as a machinist and handyman. He would go on what my mother's sister called "benders"—drinking binges that could last for days. He drank so heavily that he lost custody of his daughters on several occasions. They were taken to Catholic orphanages or foster homes. His alcoholism caused a rupture with his extended family, who all disappeared from my mother's life.

When my mother reached adolescence, he faced another problem: My mother started showing signs of mental illness.

Schizophrenia symptoms typically start in women in their late twenties. But a rare form occurs in pre-adolescence, I learned after reading more about the illness. My mother started to exhibit signs of paranoia and bursts of aggression when she was a pre-teen. She'd express joy at seeing someone one day but act as if she didn't know or care to know them the next day. When she was about thirteen, she cornered her father in the kitchen with a knife when he wouldn't give her money to go to the movies.

My grandfather had lost his wife to mental illness; now he could see the same signs in his older daughter. Did he talk about his fear? Did he try to prepare his other daughter?

None of that, Aunt Mary said when I asked those questions. She told me that he was a quiet, almost timid man who spent his spare time reading Zane Grey western novels and Catholic prayer books while chewing tobacco. He never talked about his wife's mental illness or what was happening to his older daughter.

"You had to drag words out of him," Aunt Mary said.

Nor did my mother express alarm at or awareness of what was

happening to her. Everyone treated the subject of mental illness with silence.

"We didn't talk about those things," Aunt Mary said. "Nobody talked about mental illness then. Now everybody shares everything. I don't know what your mom felt."

My mother and her sister ended up living a childhood that was just as chaotic as mine. Between their father's drinking and their mother's illness, my mother lived in four orphanages and one foster home by the time she was fifteen.

Most of these family details came out in letters and occasional phone conversations, so much so that I soon grudgingly started calling her Aunt Mary. She related all these details with a clinical detachment, never expressing much emotion about the memories I asked her to relive. It was the same emotional detachment I exhibited when asked to talk about my childhood.

But I didn't keep talking to Aunt Mary only because I wanted a guided tour of my family's genealogy. I still wanted something more: an apology and an explanation for her absence. After several years of polite letters and conversations, I decided one afternoon to be direct during a phone conversation: "Why did you take so long to get in touch with us? Was it because we're Black?"

There was silence on the other end of the line. She finally spoke in a calm, measured tone. "It wasn't because you were Black," she said. "It was because you weren't Catholic."

Bullshit, I thought.

She went on. She said my mother's family were devout Irish Catholics. They were brainwashed as kids not to play with other kids who weren't Catholic or who were Black. She said my grandfather objected to my father's courtship of my mother not because he was Black but because he was much older than my mother and because my grandfather thought my father was trying to take advantage of my mother's incipient mental illness.

I said nothing, because I didn't want to argue. I wanted to leave my mother's side of the family behind. I said goodbye, hung up, and called Pat.

"Can you believe what she said?" I asked after recounting the conversation. "Her father called our father a nigger and assaulted him. We're her blood, her nephews, and she waited until now to contact us? And none of that has to do with racism? That's bullshit!"

"Hey, it doesn't matter," Pat told me. "Just let it go."

Aunt Mary must have sensed my hostility, because she wrote me follow-up letters to explain her behavior and her father's.

My maternal grandfather didn't like my dad because of their clashing personalities, she said. "Aside from racial or religious differences, I believe your granddad and your dad's personalities clashed—only an assumption on my part since I never witnessed them together. Granddad was soft-spoken and somewhat timid. On the occasions I spoke with your dad, he seemed to be confident and outspoken. Sometimes the two don't mix."

In another follow-up letter, Aunt Mary explained why she had waited so long to contact us. To reduce it to racism, in her eyes, was simplistic.

Consider her struggles, she said. She had lost her mother to mental illness when she was a girl, then her older sister. The time she spent in foster homes was filled with loneliness and anger. When she did find some brief patches of domestic stability with her father, he gave most of his attention to my mom because she was his favorite and because she was ill.

Aunt Mary said she had faith, but by the time she became a young woman, she was filled with anger at God. Mental illness had destroyed her family. Where was God in all of that? Her childhood had made it difficult for her to get close to anyone when she became an adult.

"It's probably one of the reasons I didn't reach out to you earlier," she said. "I was just thinking of survival."

That was not enough for me. Her inability to admit that racism had *anything* to do with how my father was treated, or her absence from my life, angered me. And where were the other members of my mother's family?

I stopped calling her, and I stopped writing her.

But she continued to write me, trying to establish a bond.

"Write when you get a chance," she wrote in one letter. "I hope you received my first letter. I'm not sure if I put the proper postage on it. May God's love and protection be with you always."

Another letter: "I need to close for now, but I hope we can keep in contact. I will write soon."

Before long I stopped opening her letters and instead put them in a Tupperware box under my desk at home.

It may seem that I was unduly harsh to Aunt Mary. But there was another reason I was so angry with her from the beginning. She had bad timing. Her rationalizations reminded me of what I was experiencing in one of my first jobs as a journalist.

I didn't want to shake her hand when I met her, because her absence from my life reminded me of the most depressing experience I'd had as a journalist. It took place not long after I moved to Los Angeles in 1989.

Los Angeles was also not what I expected. As someone who grew up amid the bleak industrial landscape of inner-city Baltimore, I was enchanted with the city during visits to Susan's family.

The spell didn't last as I settled into the city after college. Los Angeles was a mishmash of tacky strip malls painted in pink and lime pastels, tanned people walking around in acid-washed jeans and blond mullets, and Mexican immigrants selling oranges at stoplights. A metallic-colored haze always seemed to cover the skyline.

There was a numbing *Groundhog Day* sameness to living in a place where every day was sunny and seventy degrees and no one could mark the passage of time through the change of seasons.

My first job was as a reporter for the *Los Angeles Daily News,* then a conservative paper in the San Fernando Valley. It had no interest in covering the Black and Latino residents in its community. I was one of a handful of Black reporters in a noisy newsroom that was led almost exclusively by white male editors. My first job was as a cop reporter, monitoring the police scanner late at night for potential news stories. Whenever I heard a police officer call in a "Code 187," I perked up. That code meant murder, and that often meant running out to my car and driving to a crime scene to interview grieving relatives of a victim.

One night while I was on scanner duty, my editor, a skinny young white guy with thick silver glasses and khakis he always wore too tight, moseyed up to my desk and gave me advice. "If a murder victim isn't white or a homeowner, we're not going to be interested," he told me. He stifled a yawn, then returned to his desk.

I was too stunned—and afraid—to say anything.

I got a new job a year later at another Los Angeles newspaper. I wanted to work closer to the city and be around more Black and Latino people. I was the first reporter on duty in the morning, and by default, I ended up covering most of the gang shootings in South Central Los Angeles, a predominantly Black inner-city area. South Central was the epicenter of one of the worst crime waves this nation has ever seen. It was a struggle for turf and money between warring Black gangs called the Crips and the Bloods. The violence was fueled by the rise of crack cocaine and amplified by the introduction of assault rifles.

I had to learn to never wear blue (Crips color) or red (Bloods color) when I went to South Central. A person could get killed in a drive-by shooting for wearing the wrong color. I started covering gangs in 1990—the same year gang-related killings in Los Angeles County had surged to a record 570 victims.[2] (Baltimore made headlines when it recorded 337 murders for 2021.)[3] The violence was so horrific that it spawned its own musical genre: gangsta rap. I covered the rise of a rap group out of Compton called N.W.A. (Niggaz Wit Attitudes).

The way the Los Angeles Police Department responded to this surging violence was almost as criminal as the acts themselves. The LAPD was a pioneer in the militarization of the nation's police.[4] It was one of the first police forces to use a helicopter, a SWAT team, and an armored personnel carrier on drug raids. It even purchased a grenade launcher. It was headed at that time by the notorious Daryl Gates, a U.S. Navy veteran who ran the LAPD like a paramilitary operation and treated Black South Central residents as enemy combatants. Gates once said that drug users "ought to be taken out and shot"[5] and that large numbers of Black people died from LAPD choke holds because their "veins or arteries do not open up as fast as they do in normal people."[6]

I ended up covering the Rodney King riots in 1992. I wasn't surprised when South Central erupted in violent protests after four white police officers were acquitted of using excessive force after striking King—a passenger in a car pulled over for speeding—fifty-six times with billy clubs as he crawled on the ground with his hands spread. On the day the protests began, I was with a gaggle of reporters in downtown Los Angeles when a petrified King went on live television and stammered, "Can we all get along?"

Covering the murders of one Black person after another every week took a toll. After covering the funeral of an eight-year-old Black girl in Watts who was killed by a stray bullet during a gang shoot-out (gang members called people killed by stray bullets "mushrooms"—things you just stepped on), I went home to my apartment in West Los Angeles and told my roommate and friend Sheldon, "There's no way people would accept this many white kids being killed in one place."

Several weeks later, I had my worst experience in South Central.

I was dispatched one morning to cover yet another gang shooting. This one had happened near the campus of the University of California. I pulled up in a neighborhood that looked like many in South Central: deceptively idyllic with neat stucco ranch homes, driveways, and palm trees dotting the streets. After exiting my car, I was walking down the sidewalk to find people to interview when I noticed something in the gutter: a smashed stroller with shell casings scattered alongside it—and dried-up bloodstains.

There had been a running gang battle the day before that forced neighborhood residents to dive for cover or flee their homes. Several people were killed, including a child pushed by her mother in a stroller. I spotted a Black man with a short Afro and wispy mustache eyeing me, so I walked over to him and introduced myself. He motioned me to a nearby apartment, which was his home.

When I went inside, his wife and several children warily greeted me. Once I sat down and started asking him about the shooting, his words poured out. He said the echo of automatic rifles rang throughout the neighborhood as gang members used

AK-47 assault rifles to shoot at one another from sidewalks and cars.

"It was like the AK Corral," he said, making a play on the word *OK*.

"What's it like living in here day to day?" I asked him, taking out my reporter's pad and microcassette recorder. More stories of violence poured out. His wife came into the living room to offer her own stories, followed by their children.

As they talked, I noticed something odd. I was sitting on the sofa, but the man and his family sat on the floor though their living room was filled with furniture.

Why am I the only one sitting in a chair? I wondered.

I glanced out one of their front windows and fumbled my pen when I noticed something about their living room walls: They were pockmarked with bullet holes. Gang members had fired so many stray bullets into the home during their time in the apartment that they now lived like moles. They moved through their home by sliding or ducking under the window openings. I even noticed that a mattress in a nearby bedroom was on the floor.

I grabbed my pen, slid off the couch, and sat on the floor with them.

After our interview ended, the man's son offered to walk me to my car. He was seventeen years old, slim with baggy black shorts and braided brown hair. As we walked to the car, he told me he had a girlfriend several blocks away. "I hardly ever see her because swine live there," he said. *Swine* was the term he used for rival gang members.

He told me that most of his friends had been killed. He couldn't imagine living much longer. He then looked at me quizzically, asking where I had gone to college and how I had gotten a job. I wasn't that much older than he was. He leaned against a streetlight as the sun struck his braids and he said something that left me fumbling for a response. "All I know is that I want to make a baby before I die."

Here was a young man who had seen so much death that he couldn't imagine living much past seventeen. I didn't know what to say.

He was part of the reason I was so angry with Aunt Mary.

As a kid, when I saw that white officer beat the Black woman in Aunt Fannie's yard, I thought of racism only as white people doing bad things to Black people. I thought racism was driven by hatred. South Central taught me that wasn't always true. Racism was also driven by indifference.

So many Black people died in South Central because white people simply didn't care. They ignored this astronomical level of violence because it wasn't affecting their kids. The Black kids, like the young man I talked to, were invisible. He was easy to ignore.

To this day, I'd rather deal with a white person who hates me than one who ignores me. At least one of them sees me as a person worthy of their emotions and energy. To refuse to acknowledge someone's existence is a special kind of cruelty.

If Pat and I had been Aunt Mary's blond, blue-eyed nephews, I doubt we would have waited until our mid-twenties to hear from her. And if she had contacted us and said she wasn't equipped or wasn't willing to be in our lives, at least I would have had some contact with my mother's family.

I couldn't look into Aunt Mary's heart to figure out if she ever hated us because we were half-Black. But she did something worse in my eyes: She ignored us for all those years. Not a call, not a letter. Nothing.

. . .

But I had another aunt who never ignored me. I received a call around this time from Aunt Sylvia. She wanted to visit.

I left Los Angeles in the early 1990s and landed a job with *The Atlanta Journal-Constitution,* one of the largest newspapers in the South. I was tired of covering gangs and seeing Black people carted off in body bags from gang shootings. I wanted to see trauma-free Blackness. Atlanta was the place. I covered education and moved on to the civil rights beat. Atlanta—dubbed "the cradle of the civil rights movement"—was the birthplace of the Reverend Martin Luther King, Jr., and the headquarters of many Black political and business institutions that supported the civil rights movement. After South Central, it was a relief to walk through downtown Atlanta and see so many sharply dressed Black professionals and interview civil rights legends like John Lewis and Andrew Young instead of "Eight Ball" and "Stab Happy" from the Crips and the Bloods.

Something else I was thrilled about was Aunt Sylvia's visit on my first Thanksgiving in Atlanta. She arrived one chilly Saturday morning on an Amtrak train following a fifteen-hour trip from Baltimore. I drove to the station in midtown Atlanta to pick her up. After the Amtrak lurched into the station, passengers wrapped in thick sweaters and scarves exited the train, pulling suitcases and hugging family members waiting for them on the platform. Pigeons milled about the platform, pecking for crumbs, and someone made an announcement on the intercom. It seemed like all the passengers had disembarked before I spotted her at the end of the platform, standing alone by the train with her suitcases.

I jogged up to her to help her with her bags. She dropped them on the platform and gave me a bemused smile, the same kind she would give me when she was tickled by something I did.

"Hi, Aunt Sylvia," I said.

"How's my baby?" she said, hugging me tight.

"I got your bags," I said, picking them up. Then we headed to my car.

Aunt Sylvia had always been a slow walker, but this time every step seemed to require effort. She didn't have her wig on, and her hair seemed thinner and drier. Even her eyes seemed cloudy behind her glasses, and her body had lost its stoutness.

I ignored what I saw and kept chatting as she and I walked to my car.

I drove her to my cousin Carolyn's home in suburban Atlanta, where Aunt Sylvia had decided to stay. Carolyn was a corporate lawyer with a palatial home more than big enough to fit my other cousins and us on Sunday for Thanksgiving dinner. When dinner was ready, we all sat at the table, but I noticed Aunt Sylvia's chair was empty.

"I'll get her," I told Carolyn. I pushed away from the table and ran upstairs.

I knocked on the guest bedroom, where Aunt Sylvia was staying. "Aunt Sylvia?"

"Come on in," she said softly.

She was sitting on the edge of the bed, bent over at the waist. She looked up and gave me a weary smile, then leaned back and started to reminisce. She talked about taking Pat and me to church and seeing us graduate and joked that I was still "Repeating John," the boy who always had to ask why.

I nodded, tapping my hands loudly against my thighs. I was hungry and knew everyone was already gathered at the table.

"They're waiting for us downstairs, Aunt Sylvia," I said.

She opened her mouth as if she were about to say something. Then she shooed the thought away with a shake of her head and instead held out her hand. I helped her rise from the bed and led her downstairs. It was a fun and lively dinner where we all reminisced about the big family dinners Aunt Sylvia used to take Pat and me to when we were kids.

After dinner ended, I thanked Carolyn for hosting us, said my goodbyes, and headed back to my place. Two days later, I drove Aunt Sylvia to the Amtrak station, where I hugged her goodbye and told her I'd come to Baltimore soon to visit her.

When spring arrived, Pat called me to say Aunt Sylvia was sick and in the hospital. "It's serious," he said after a heavy sigh. "I don't know if she's going to make it."

I flew to Baltimore the next day, but I did something unexpected after checking in to my hotel. I didn't immediately go to the hospital to see her. Instead, I visited an old tennis coach, then a high school buddy. The next day I had lunch with a college classmate. I kept finding excuses not to visit Aunt Sylvia.

Three days after arriving, I finally drove to the hospital in downtown Baltimore to see her. I walked into the intensive-care unit, where I found her alone in her hospital room, lying in bed with her eyes closed. The curtains of the window were open, and ribbons of sunlight streamed into the room. I stood at the entrance of the room, closed my eyes, and looked upward to gather myself. I then walked to the side of her bed.

She was still as her chest rose and fell with shallow breaths. Her once plump, sturdy figure had shriveled, and her dark skin had yellowed. The hospital staff had attached monitoring wires to her arms, and a heart monitor beeped in the silence.

I pulled a chair from the corner of the room and slid it next to her bed, then sat down and leaned forward so that I could touch her shoulder, just to feel her warmth.

She didn't stir.

I didn't know what to do. So I started peppering her with questions like I had as a kid, when she called me "Repeating John."

"Aunt Sylvia, I got a new girlfriend, but I think I'm too young to get married. What do you think?"

I lowered my head, then looked at her again. "I'm sorry I took so long to visit," I said quietly. "I don't know what's wrong with me. . . ."

Her eyelids fluttered. Then she opened her eyes and looked at me. A flicker of a smile appeared on her face, and her eyes brightened. It was the same look she would give me when I'd ask a silly question or do something that made her proud.

She closed her eyes again.

"Aunt Sylvia? Aunt Sylvia?" I said.

But her eyes remained closed, her breathing rhythmic but shallow. I sat and looked at her. Her eyes didn't open again. A nurse, I think, came into the room, then left. Still, I kept looking at Aunt Sylvia. Finally I stood up and stroked her hands, the same hands that had tucked me into bed on those cold nights in Baltimore and placed water jars under our covers for warmth.

I gazed one more time at her face. Then I turned and walked out of the room.

Aunt Sylvia died of liver failure at Maryland General Hospital several days after my visit. She was sixty years old.

Her funeral was held at New Shiloh Baptist Church in West Baltimore, a church she had recently joined, which was three blocks away from where she had helped raise Pat and me. It was a muggy, sticky Monday afternoon in August. I met Patrick in the foyer along with some other relatives.

The service went by in a blur. A soloist sang one of Aunt Sylvia's favorite hymns, "Blessed Assurance," and the preacher delivered a eulogy. I didn't hear any of it. I looked over at Patrick. He was supposed to deliver some remarks, but as I watched him bury his head in his hands to softly cry, I wondered if he would be able to do it. When the time came for him to go up to the front, he jabbed my thigh without raising his head. "You do it," he said.

The church was silent as I scooted out of the pew and walked to the pulpit at the front of the church. I stood in front of the microphone, sighed, and looked out into the audience. I saw Twiggy, my older brother, lean forward in the pew and look at me anxiously.

I don't remember much of what I said, but I did something I had never done before. I mentioned my mother publicly, in front of my family and childhood friends who had come to pay their respects.

I slowed my breathing. "As some of you know," I said, "Pat and I didn't grow up with our mother. It was tough at times. We didn't even know who our mother was, but we did have Aunt Sylvia."

I thought of turning to my right to look at Aunt Sylvia's body, but I dared not. I knew I'd break down.

I couldn't think of anything else to say, so I stepped away from the microphone, returned to the pew, and sat down next to Pat. He reached out and grabbed my hand, and I squeezed his.

The ride to the cemetery was quiet. When we arrived, Pat and I helped carry Aunt Sylvia's coffin to the gravesite, which was two rows down from her mother, Daisy Cora Lee, my paternal grandmother. I couldn't remember Grandma Daisy. She died when I was three. But people told me that she and I were inseparable. I have a home movie taken just before her death where she was leading Pat and me through an amusement park. We followed her like ducklings tailing their mother. When she sat down, we raised our hands, pleading for her to pick us up. She smiled, rose, and took our hands, then walked us to another amusement ride.

I was told that when my mother was taken away, there was talk of putting us up for adoption. But my grandmother stepped in and said, "No. We're going to do this. I love them. We're going to take care of them."

I now stood before the gravesite of two Black women—one I could no longer remember and one I could never forget—both of whom had saved me.

A preacher delivered more remarks at the gravesite. I didn't listen. The sun was high in the sky, and I wiped sweat from my brow. After the graveside services ended, friends and colleagues of Aunt Sylvia approached Pat and me to offer their condolences. One stranger was a young man who gave us a huge smile and a bear hug like he had known us all our lives.

"You gotta be John and Pat, right?"

"Yeah," I said.

"I feel like I know you because your aunt talked about you all the time. It was always 'My boys this. My boys that.'"

As the well-wishers melted away to return to their cars, Pat and I remained at Aunt Sylvia's gravesite. The cemetery was now silent, save for the roar of a passenger jet above the buzzing of cicadas. We said nothing as we looked at her coffin, now lowered into the ground.

Our champion was gone.

I placed my hand on Pat's shoulder. Then we turned and walked toward a waiting car.

Momma,
Can You Dance?

Reverend Nibs at John's wedding

stopped to listen to a chorus of birds singing in the trees above me and gaze at the yellow black-eyed Susans blooming next to the church in front of me. It was the first blush of spring, and I was about to walk into the modest brick building for Sunday morning worship. The church stood on a corner in an Atlanta neighborhood dotted with large, hand-

some, Craftsman-style houses, white picket fences, and mag-
nolia trees.

I was there for work, not worship, but it was hard not to enjoy
the tranquil setting.

It was four years after Aunt Sylvia's death, and my responsibilities
at *The Atlanta Journal-Constitution* had expanded to include writing about religion. I'd heard about an unusual church with a special pastor no more than twenty minutes from where I lived, so I
decided to visit on a Sunday to find out more.

I took a program from an usher at the front door and sat in the
back pew. An organist in the choir loft opened the service with a
rousing melody that elicited some scattered amens. After he finished, a slight, blond middle-aged man in a preacher's robe came
down from the pulpit, stood in front of the pews, and faced the
congregation with raised hands.

"For he himself is our peace, who has made the two groups
one and has destroyed the barrier, the dividing wall of hostility,"
the man said in a booming voice.[1]

The pastor returned to the pulpit to commence the service.
During a rollicking gospel hymn, I scanned the pews to study the
church members. Clean-shaven white men in suits who looked
like CEOs stood next to young Black men in dreads. A young
white couple tousled the curly hair of a Black child who was sitting in the woman's lap. A burly white man who looked like a
biker shared a hymnal with a Black woman in an African head-
band and a kente cloth.

My eyes drifted to something else above the choir loft: a large
stained-glass window depicting Jesus ascending to heaven. It had
been altered. Jesus's face had been painted brown, and two women
had been inserted into the group of eleven male disciples watching Jesus ascend.

I wrote the pastor's name in my reporter's notebook: Reverend Gibson "Nibs" Stroupe. I placed the notebook in my back pocket and left before the benediction.

I would return to this church—again and again. Nibs, and the other people at Oakhurst, would open my eyes to a world I never knew existed.

I was close to giving up on interracial churches by the time I visited Oakhurst. Part of it was because of my experiences in South Central. I couldn't find an interracial church in L.A. and ended up attending a Black congregation in South Central. Most of it, though, was because of an experience at another interracial church in Atlanta a year earlier.

When I arrived at the church, it was predominantly white, with Black members making up only about 15 percent of its congregation. More Black people joined the church as the surrounding neighborhood changed. When Black membership surged to more than half the congregation in a five-year period, white members fled. It was an ecclesiastical version of "white flight"— the term used to describe whites fleeing neighborhoods and schools when the number of Black or brown people tips over a certain ratio,[2] usually around 20 percent. Scholars who have studied multiracial congregations say white church members tend to leave a congregation when their number falls below 50 percent.[3]

The megachurch eventually became all Black, except for the white ministers who led the church. I left to attend another Black church. I was tired of segregated churches, whatever the color. I wanted to feel what I first experienced attending an interracial church while at Howard.

To research my article on Oakhurst, I left an interview request on the church's answering machine. Not long after, I got a call from Nibs. He wanted to talk over lunch. We set up a time for the next day. *Maybe this interracial church will be different,* I thought as I drove to meet him.

He asked that we meet at Piccadilly, a restaurant in a mall just outside Atlanta. He was wearing Hush Puppies, beige slacks, and a button-down shirt, and he was waiting for me when I arrived. He was the only white person in a cafeteria filled with Black people from the working-class Black neighborhood that surrounded the mall.

He smiled and extended his hand. "Thank you for getting together," he said in a twangy southern accent.

We sat at a booth, and our talked drifted to his background. He said he grew up in the Jim Crow South, spending most of his childhood in Arkansas near the Mississippi Delta. He was a teenager when the Civil Rights Movement rolled through in the 1950s and '60s. He said he was opposed to it and told me he once believed that Black people were biologically inferior, civil rights demonstrators were outside agitators, and the Reverend Martin Luther King, Jr., was a communist who just wanted people's money.

He said this all matter-of-factly between sips of sweet tea.

My eyebrows rose.

"No one ever sat down and told me that Black people were inferior," he said. "It was just in the air. We breathed it in."

"What changed you?" I asked.

He said his transformation was gradual. He watched on TV as King delivered his "I Have a Dream" speech at the Lincoln Memorial and wondered if maybe he was genuine. Later a high school teacher gave him a copy of *Cry, the Beloved Country,* a book about a Black rural minister's search for his son set against the backdrop of apartheid in South Africa. Nibs said he was touched by the pastor's kindness and earnestness and remembered looking up from the page and thinking, *Gosh, they might be like us.*

But it was a summer in Harlem, New York, that was truly transformative. After high school, Nibs enrolled in a church ministry in Tennessee that assigned him and a childhood buddy to an anti-poverty program in Harlem. There, he made friends with Black people for the first time. He even dated a Black woman.

"That changed everything," he told me. "What we were thinking when we went to Harlem was, *Let's get out of our small town and see a different world.* We weren't thinking, *Oh, let's change our minds on race.* But it was just our daily life with African American people. They acted like regular people, which was shocking at first. That was the place where I crossed over."

We talked more. What stood out to me was not just what he said but how he said it. Every question I asked was followed by an immediate response that was direct, clear, and felt genuine. He told me something that he often returned to in books and sermons. One of the reasons it's so difficult for white people to jettison racist beliefs is that for many it would be the equivalent of turning their backs on their families.

He said he learned racism not from unapologetic racists like Ku Klux Klan members. He learned racism from members of his family and his childhood church. Almost every white person learns racism from nice white people they love and trust, he said. "I know that stuff; it's in my veins. I grew up in the belly of the beast, and I'm still not free of it."

After we finished eating, I stood up to go.

Nibs picked up the check and said cheerfully, "Let's do this again."

I joined Oakhurst several months after my first lunch with Nibs. I even met with church members for lunch and dinner and dropped by the church's Monday night Bible study, where I participated in spirited discussions about the Bible and current events. I started making friends.

I was now part of a celebrity church that was routinely featured in publications like *Time* magazine[4] and *The Christian Science Monitor* and on National Public Radio. Most of the headlines told the same story: Here was a multiracial and multicultural church where white members shared pews and power with Black and brown members. The pulpit showcased at least one woman or person of color at every Sunday service. The worship style included traditional elements of the Presbyterian church alongside those of the Black church, such as up-tempo gospel songs and a tradition from my childhood church: testimony time. There, testimony time was called "the sharing of joys and concerns." But it was the same: spontaneous stories from people in the pews.

There was another part of Oakhurst's story that virtually every journalist got wrong. We were depicted as this sunny multiracial church where everybody got along. One *Time* magazine journalist described the atmosphere as one of "equanimity" and "heavenly" music.[5] That was a fairy tale. We had constant debates over race, gender issues, and money. We clashed over issues such as the mission statement, the affirmation of gay and lesbian members, and what music to play.

One of these clashes could have torn the church apart. It involved a tense encounter between Nibs and Inez, a Black church elder. Inez was an outspoken leader, a family counselor who talked openly about how difficult it was for her to accept a white man like Nibs as her spiritual leader.

The story of their encounter became an unofficial part of the church's history, something Nibs used to illustrate how difficult it was for him to share power.

Inez called Nibs one night because she was concerned about a decision he had made. As they talked, the conversation grew more animated.

"Why are you angry?" Nibs asked Inez.

"What makes you think I'm angry?"

"You sound mad."

"No, I'm not angry. Believe me, if I was angry, you would know it."

There was silence on the phone.

Inez then told Nibs that she thought she knew why he said she was angry.

"Are you willing to receive it?" she said.

Nibs pondered for a minute, then said, "Okay, let's hear it."

"I'm guessing that you as a white man in power are not accustomed to having a Black person treat you as a peer, and you are not accustomed to having a Black woman stand up to you. My treating you as an equal is something that makes you angry, and instead of owning up to that, you project your anger onto me. Is that right?"

Nibs was quiet before finally saying, "Yes, I think you may be right. I am in uncharted territory here."

What Inez said next stunned him again. "Now we can work with this," she said. "As long as I know that you know and that you will occasionally acknowledge your racism, we can work together. You may be surprised at your racism, but I am not, and none of the Black people at Oakhurst are surprised either."

Inez became one of Nibs's most important allies at Oakhurst. They went on to write books together and give lectures on racism, with both sharing the story of that call.

These kinds of conversations between members happened all the time at Oakhurst. Nibs was no white savior—he was converted by the Black and brown people he met at Oakhurst, not the other way around. Inez was as much of a leader at Oakhurst as Nibs.

But it's something that Nibs wrote about that conversation that really stuck with me. After discussing the confrontation in his book, he wrote, "It is not the responsibility of people of color to engage me or change me—that responsibility belongs to me and to all of us who are classified as 'white.' And I cannot say it often enough—all of us who are classified as 'white' are captive to this power . . . and we must all go on this journey in some form or fashion."[6]

After several years of attending Oakhurst, my time at the church took another unexpected turn. I was invited to become an elder. I accepted, which was something I would have never imagined for myself.

I was joking with Nibs one day when I told him, chuckling, "You know, you restored my hope in white people."

I found another source of hope during this time in my life. It started when a co-worker approached me with a smile one day and said, "I know somebody you should meet."

A week later, I found myself sitting alone at a vegetarian restaurant in Atlanta, waiting for the woman to show. And waiting. Almost thirty minutes had passed since the time we'd agreed on for lunch. I was just about to leave when I saw her walk in. She had shoulder-length curly brown hair, a fashion model's perfect smile, and eyes that seemed to be either green or hazel—they were unlike any I'd seen before.

"I'm sorry, I'm sorry," she said as she approached the table. "I had the wrong directions."

John with his wife, Terry

I stood up and pulled a seat out for her, and we shook hands.

We moved easily into a conversation that went past the lunch hour. Her name was Terrylynn Pons, and she had recently graduated from one of the top seminaries in the United States, Emory University's Candler School of Theology. She was working as the executive director of a pre-school ministry for a large Methodist church in Atlanta.

I wish I could say I gave a good first impression. But I bombarded her with questions about her personal life while I parried all her attempts to get me to talk about my childhood or my parents. I was self-conscious about having a mother who had a mental illness. I didn't think a woman would consider me good dating material if I told her about my mother. During a previous relationship, I had told the woman about my mom. When I broke it off, she left me a voicemail saying that she was too good for me anyway and added, "At least I don't have a mother who's crazy."

When our lunch date ended, I offered to walk Terrylynn to her car. She politely declined but said she hoped to meet again. As I walked to my car, I thought, *I could marry this woman.*

That lunch was just the first of many dates.

Terrylynn, or "Terry" as I would soon call her, was different. From our first date, I instinctively felt that I could trust her. Part of it came from what I could glean about her upbringing. She was a native of Guatemala and the oldest daughter of two missionaries who'd done what my parents had done—they violated the social norms to be together. Her father was a white Hispanic man who scandalized his family by marrying Erenie, a Black woman from the Bahamas who was also part indigenous. Terry knew what it was like to grow up different from others. She told me she was often taunted by the children she went to school with because her lighter skin and curly hair made her stand out.

We were married a year later in the Methodist church where she worked.

Wedding music played as I walked down the aisle in a black tux to wait for my bride, while Patrick, my best man, walked alongside me. Nibs stood at the front of the church, holding a Bible and smiling, ready to officiate our wedding ceremony.

After saying our vows, Terry and I walked hand in hand outside and down the church steps, past our family and friends, who had formed a line to cheer and shower us with rice. I immediately saw a familiar face smiling at me in the crowd. My father stood there, beaming, in a smart navy-blue suit set off by a dark-red silk tie.

There was one family member, though, who wasn't there: my mother. I had decided not to fly her to Atlanta. I told myself that it was because Mom was too ill, but I knew there was another reason: I was ashamed. I didn't want to explain my mom to friends

John with his father on his wedding day

and co-workers. Better to keep that side of my life secret, I concluded.

I was older, but I still hadn't quite gotten over the sadness of
meeting my mom in a mental institution. Even when she was in
group homes, I could never get used to visiting her. Those places
were all run by people who were paid by a combination of Social
Security disability benefits, Medicaid, and subsidies from Baltimore's Department of Social Services. Pat and I briefly talked
about moving Mom to private care, but those costs could range
from $10,000 to $60,000 a month. The homes Mom was in were
usually neat and tidy, but they also included other people with
mental illnesses who would come and interrupt our conversations, sometimes asking for cigarettes or introducing themselves.
Their loneliness was palpable. Few of those people had anyone to
visit them.

I started visiting my mom at the group homes out of duty. But the visits never seemed to become routine for her. When I rang the doorbell, I'd often hear my mom stir in the background. I'd walk inside and see her half trotting and half shuffling to me with the same look of astonished joy she had given me at Crownsville. "Oh boy! Oh boy! I'm so happy!"

On each visit, the same ritual would unfold. We'd sit down on the couch and she'd ask for Pepsi, a Saint Jude medal, and money. She'd refer to Crownsville: "I'm so glad I'm out of the crazy house." And she would make light of her illness. She'd stop in mid-conversation and jokingly say, "Don't mind me. I'm crazy."

Once, I gave her some money and watched as she looked over her shoulder and then stuffed the money in her bra.

"Mom," I said. "What do you need money for? We send you money for everything you need."

She looked at me and whispered, "For hard times. Hard times."

I later learned that putting money in her bra was a habit she had picked up in asylums like Crownsville. She hid money because patients and hospital staff stole what few possessions she had. She hid so many of her possessions under her pillow at night that it often looked like she was sitting up.

When I'd rise to leave, she'd say the same thing: "Pray for me, John."

"I always do, Mom," I'd say, hugging her. "I always do."

When I left those visits, I didn't feel like talking to anyone for a while. I made a living talking to strangers, but I couldn't talk to my mom like I wanted. I didn't want anyone to see this side of my life, even Terry. It made me feel helpless. I usually drove away from those visits feeling emotionally drained and despondent.

I waited four years to introduce Terry to my mom. The day we headed to see Mom, I expected to leave our visit with the same sense of sadness I usually carried. But this time proved to be better than I'd hoped.

On a sunny spring day, I drove with TL to a daycare center in an industrial park in suburban Maryland because my mother went to the daycare several times a week with other members of her group home. It offered games, dance classes, and other activities for people with mental illnesses. Pat was waiting for me when we drove up. He and I both preferred to meet our mom at the daycare to get away from the dreary atmosphere of the group home.

When I walked to the daycare's entrance this time, I noticed someone sitting inside with my mother. It was my father, puffing away on a cigarette.

"Hey, Dad," I said as I walked inside. He gruffly greeted me.

"Let's go outside," I said, knowing that the daycare didn't allow smoking inside.

We all walked outside and sat in some folding chairs just outside the entrance. My father had on a raggedy USMC camouflage cap, a brown flannel shirt, and black jeans with grease stains on his left thigh. Mom was dressed in a smart pink knit cap, a striped blue-and-white blouse, and blue slacks, and her thick silver hair was cut close in a cropped pixie cut.

My father plucked another Pall Mall cigarette from a packet in his pocket and lit it. As he began to banter with my mother, a young Black man who was a member of the group home walked up to my father and looked at my mom. "Shirley, can I have a cigarette?"

My mom was generous to a fault. When we sent her money, she gave most of it away to other residents at the group home. She did the same with the coffee, clothes, and other gifts we sent.

"Tony, give him a cigarette," she said.

My father ignored her and kept puffing away.

"Tony," my mother said as she looked at him sternly. He looked at her, annoyed, and sighed. My mother raised her left eyebrow and stared at him. His shoulders slumped, and he handed a cigarette to the stranger.

"Thank you," the man said with a big smile.

My father glumly smoked as my mother looked at him, giving him an almost-imperceptible nod.

As our visit ended, I walked to the car to get some Saint Jude prayer books for Mom. My parents followed. My dad leaned against the car and handed a cigarette to my mom. They started to talk about how they liked to go out to dance and listen to Tony Bennett.

I was in a playful mood because I hardly ever saw my parents together. So I said, "Momma, can you dance?"

She smiled, did a little shimmy of her hips, and looked at my father. They both laughed.

This is so cool, I thought as I watched them laugh together.

My mother then broke into one of her favorite Tony Bennett songs, a full-throated rendition in the parking lot, not caring who heard: "*I left my heart in San Francisco! High on a hill, it calls to me. . . .*"

My father lowered his head in mock embarrassment.

I looked at Pat. He had a goofy grin on his face and looked back at me with raised eyebrows.

Pat asked them how they met.

"Yeah, I was nineteen," Mom said.

Pat feigned horror and looked at Dad. "You contributed to the delinquency of my momma?"

My father chuckled as he watched Mom break into another jig after finishing her song.

"How about me?" he said. "Ain't she contributing to the delinquency of me? Or am I too far gone?"

I watched the scene, drinking it in. I continued to stare at them for so long TL sidled up next to me.

"What do you think?" she asked.

"This is the first time I've seen them like this," I said.

"Well, what do you think about it?"

"I don't know. I don't know," I said as I continued to watch my mother and father banter.

To anyone else, the scene would have been unremarkable. Not for me. To see my parents laughing and affectionately teasing each other was a revelation. *Maybe,* I thought as I looked at my dad, *he really does care for her.*

Terry and I exchanged hugs with Mom and said goodbye. Then we said goodbye to Pat and my father. I drove away, but this time there was a smile on my face.

There was still one family member, though, who didn't bring a smile to my face: Mom's sister, Aunt Mary. I hadn't invited her to my wedding, and I kept my distance from her in subsequent years.

Two years after getting married, I wrote my first book, called *Children of the Movement.* I profiled the adult children of the most recognizable figures in the Civil Rights Movement, including leading figures like Martin Luther King, Jr., martyrs like James Earl Chaney, segregationists like George Wallace, and Black Panther leaders like Elaine Brown.

I wrote it because I wanted to know what it was like to be the child of a civil rights icon like King or Malcolm X—or the child of the notorious segregationist George Wallace. One of my favorite parts of writing the book was telling the stories of how the children of segregationists like Wallace reconciled with their fathers' enemies.

One of my first book signings took place at a Barnes & Noble in downtown Baltimore. During a phone call, I'd told Aunt Mary about the signing but thought nothing more of it. As I took my place in front of the small audience at the bookstore, I saw her standing at the back of the crowd, near the store's entrance.

She smiled at me when I made eye contact. I nodded and launched into my presentation for the crowd who'd formed to hear me talk.

Later, after my talk, I sat at a table to sign books. As a line formed, TL came up beside me and glanced toward Aunt Mary, who was still standing at the back of the crowd. "Is that your aunt?" she whispered.

"Yeah," I said while I signed a book for someone.

"Let me bring her to you," TL said.

"No, she can wait," I said without looking up.

TL sighed and wove through the crowd to say hello to my mother's sister. I had never introduced her to my aunt nor talked much about her. I watched as TL gave her a big hug.

"You must be Terry," Aunt Mary said.

"Have you been here the whole time?" TL asked.

They chatted for a while; then the conversation trailed off.

"I just want to say hello to him," Aunt Mary finally said.

"Give me a minute," TL said. "Let me go over and let him know you're here. I don't know that he's seen you."

TL returned to me as I talked with some people in the crowd. "I just met your aunt," she whispered in my ear. "She's been waiting a long time to talk to you."

"Let her wait," I said. I was still focused on signing books.

After the line thinned out, I looked up to see Aunt Mary still standing in the same spot. I walked up to her. "Thank you for coming," I said.

She reached out to hug me. I gave her a mechanical pat on the back and pulled away. She stood for a minute, saying nothing, and then she turned to TL with a smile. "It was very nice to meet you," she said.

I nodded at my mother's sister again. The manager of the bookstore tapped me on the shoulder. There were some latecomers who wanted to hear my presentation. Did I have time to talk to them?

"Sure," I said. I turned and walked toward the newcomers, who were waiting for me at the table with my books.

I didn't turn to say goodbye to Aunt Mary. I was too focused on retelling one of my favorite stories in the book. It was about the daughter of a notorious segregationist governor who ended up befriending a civil rights activist her father had opposed.

I ended the story by making the same point I always made after giving my presentation: "We must," I'd solemnly declare to my audience, "learn to forgive our enemies."

I don't know what Aunt Mary thought when she heard that story, but she kept reaching out to me for at least the next five years. She wrote letters and sent birthday cards and family mementos. I didn't open them or quickly scanned them before placing them in the plastic container under my desk.

By this time in my mid-thirties, I was burned out on race. I wished I could place the subject of racism in a box and lock it away. I wrote about it constantly for my job. I lived it with the white members of my family. I wanted to move on.

But there was still someone who wouldn't let me.

It started off like any other night. When I dragged myself to bed, TL was already asleep. I'm a light sleeper who awakens at the slightest noise, but that night I slept through. When I awakened the next morning, my T-shirt was soaked with sweat. So were the sheets. I rubbed my eyes, turned to TL, and saw that she was already sitting up in bed. Her blouse was soaked as well, and her eyes were wide with fear. She looked at me like she was going to burst into tears.

"There was a man in here last night," she said.

"What?"

"You didn't see him?"

"What man? What are you talking about?"

The fear in her voice turned to agitation. She held her hands up in exasperation. "I woke up last night, and I saw a man standing over you at the side of the bed, looking down at you."

My heart thumped, and I felt a familiar chill sweep through my body.

"What man?" I asked, hoping TL didn't hear the quiver in my voice.

She said that she was awakened by something and saw a well-dressed man with thick white hair in our bedroom. He stood over the bed just inches away from me, peering down at me with a furrowed brow.

Fuck, I thought. I propped myself up in the bed and threw my pillow behind me.

"I tried to waken you, but you wouldn't wake up," TL said, her voice breaking. "I kept saying, 'John, wake up, wake up,' but you wouldn't. You left me alone."

She burst out sobbing.

I hugged her.

I had told TL about my mother and Aunt Mary, but I had never mentioned their father. I jumped out of bed, padded into my office, and looked under the desk for the plastic container. I reached inside and pulled out a photograph. Then I returned to the bed, where TL still sat, and showed her the photo.

"Does this look like the man?"

She looked at the photograph, and then she turned to me, her brow furrowed in confusion. Her voice took on an angry edge. "Where did you get this picture? Who is he?"

"Is this the man?" I repeated.

"Yes," she said. "Who is he? What is he to you?"

I flopped back in the bed, wondering what the hell was going on.

I sighed and looked at Terry. I took her hands in mine. "He's my grandfather," I said. "He's my mother's father."

Talking to the Dead

William "Bill" Dailey,
John's maternal grandfather

T erry stared at me as we both sat upright in bed, clothes
soaked, clutching each other's hands.

"What do you mean?" she asked me. "Your grandfather?"

I looked away, trying to figure out how I'd tell her this story. I
had never talked to her about my grandfather or his ghostly visitation when I was a kid. I had been determined to forget it. It
wasn't the type of story I'd bring up over a dinner date. I was
afraid, if I told her such a story, she'd assume that the mental illness that had taken over my mom had been passed down to me.

I didn't even talk to Pat about what we had seen as kids. The memory was traumatic to both of us.

Now I had to relive it.

I told Terry about my grandfather's visit and how Pat and I had discovered his identity.

"I don't know why this is happening," I said.

Maybe it didn't really happen, I thought.

"You sure you weren't dreaming?" I asked her. "What did he look like? Did he say anything? Are you sure you were awake?"

Terry stared at me in disbelief and angrily dropped my hands when I started questioning her, implying that she had imagined everything. I shut up.

We eventually tossed our wet clothes into the hamper and went on with our day. But I kept pestering her for days, asking her more questions that implied she had imagined the entire incident. I wanted to convince myself that it hadn't happened. She threw up her hands in frustration about a week later when I asked her if she was sure I hadn't talked about my grandfather before.

"JB," she said, shaking her head, "I can't talk about it anymore. I'm tired."

After that, I did what I had learned how to do so well at the foster homes: I blocked it out. Weeks, months, and years went by, and I forgot all about the visit.

Besides, I had another reason to forget. I wasn't thinking much about ghosts when Terry shared her story. I was more worried about demons, the kind I was encountering in my new job.

In 2008, I was hired by CNN.com. I became the site's primary writer for race, not long after President Obama, the nation's first Black president, was sworn in. It was a time of swelling racial optimism, when people unabashedly used the word *post-racial* to describe the new era America was entering.

I had first encountered Obama when he was a community organizer in Chicago. I was assigned to cover a city hall protest when I was an intern at the *Chicago Tribune.* When I attended the protest, I was struck by the charisma of this tall young Black man with big ears and overalls who commanded the room. I distinctly remember telling myself that this guy was wasting his time as a community organizer and should go into politics.

He apparently took my unsolicited advice. I was as amazed as anyone else when I saw the photos of Black, white, and brown people shedding tears in a crowd that had gathered at Chicago's Grant Park in 2008 for Obama's victory celebration. I remember the "Yes We Can" bumper stickers and the T-shirts of Obama's portrait merged with King's. Even people who hadn't voted for Obama were moved to tears by his election. It seemed like we had entered the Promised Land.

The euphoria following Obama's election was followed by a white backlash. Much of this backlash appeared in news stories and on social media feeds. Obama was called "the primate in chief" and depicted as an African witch doctor at political rallies. First Lady Michelle Obama was depicted as a chimpanzee and called "an ape in heels." The emergence of the birther conspiracy forced the nation's first Black president to show his papers, or his birth certificate, to authenticate his identity—the same demand that free Blacks had to comply with during the slave era.

When the poet Ishmael Reed was asked to describe the impact of Obama's election, he said something that stuck with me: "All the demons of American racism are rising from the sewer."[1]

One day, those demons came for me.

I was clicking through the internet, searching for a photo that

I could use for my Facebook page, when I came across a photo of myself staring intently at the camera in front of a CNN logo. *I like this one,* I thought as I prepared to save it. I paused after looking closer at the site.

It was called Stormfront.org.[2] The language at the top of the site said its mission was to deliver "all news of interest to white nationalists" and assured them that "every month is white history month." The caption beneath my photograph read, "CNN's John Blake: 'I like to shame whites.'" Below my picture, various readers offered commentary on my CNN articles about race.

"Don't like White? Then go to Africa, you biracial ape!"

"Bet he'd not be so flippant swinging from a rope. . . ."

"I like to shame mongrels like John Blake who only got the position because of affirmative action."

Why worry about the terror that comes by night when white supremacists threaten your life by day? I had witnessed plenty of racism while growing up in Baltimore and working as a Black journalist. This was different. It was unapologetic. People were saying things publicly that they wouldn't have dared say years earlier. The racial climate in the country was changing, and as a reporter at CNN, I had a front-row seat to this transformation.

The escalating racial tension hit home for me in May 2015 when I was assigned to cover the Freddie Gray protests in Baltimore. When I arrived in my old neighborhood on a balmy Friday morning, I saw three Humvees with mounted machine guns take a position on the street where I grew up. The avenue where Aunt Sylvia had driven Pat and me to church was dotted with the charred remains of burned-out stores and cars. My heart sank when I drove by my childhood church, Union Temple Baptist Church. It was now abandoned, boarded up, and streaked with graffiti.

Everyone seemed to be on edge, walking quickly through the streets, looking over their shoulders, not saying hi to anyone. Drivers were accelerating through red lights and stop signs, fearful of being a carjacking victim if they stopped for even a moment. Everything seemed to be peeling away—the paint on the derelict homes and the social fabric that once held my community together.

I parked my rental car and knocked on the front door of the house that had been my father's. He had moved away twenty years earlier. Iron bars covered the windows. A man washing a nearby car paused, looked at me from the curb, and shouted, "She won't come to the front door. She's a little skittish."

I turned to my left and spotted a sky-blue Chevrolet Corvette Stingray sports car parked in front of the house two doors down.

It can't be, I thought. *He's still here?*

I walked to the house and knocked on the door. An older man in glasses peered at me through the screen door without opening it. His name was Herb. A smile flashed across his face, and he opened the door.

"John?" he said tentatively. "Sylvia's boy?"

"Hey, Herb," I said.

He came out on the porch, and we talked about old times and how things had changed. He said nobody talked to one another on our block anymore. Of the thirty-eight homes on the block, only seven were owned by their occupants. When his home was recently burglarized, it took three 911 calls and fifty-five minutes for the police to show up.

"I could be mutilated or lying in the street, and nobody would call the police," he said.

After we chatted a little longer, I shook Herb's hand and got into my rental car. I looked in my rearview mirror at his house.

He was still standing in the doorway, giving me a wan smile as I drove away.

I would write about my encounter with Herb for a CNN article. I tried to explain what had happened in West Baltimore. But it was hard to convey what had destroyed my neighborhood, because most people wanted to hear the same old war stories about race riots and heartless young Black men gunning one another down on corners.

The typical narratives I read about West Baltimore focused on the violence, not the causes. The stories didn't talk enough about the departure of blue-collar jobs that employed men like my father—jobs with a living wage and union benefits.

Most stories didn't talk about a whole generation of young Black men in Baltimore who had been made virtually unemployable by Baltimore mayors who took a "zero tolerance" approach to crime. They locked Black men up for everything from standing on the corner, which they called "trespassing," to nebulous infractions like "disturbing the peace." Even if those young men beat those charges, they had an arrest on their record. That's partly how my nephew Mike got caught up in the justice system, through penny-ante charges that made it more difficult for him to find housing and good jobs.

Journalists didn't talk about the isolation—physical and psychological—that comes from growing up in West Baltimore. They didn't talk enough about popular politicians like Maryland governor Larry Hogan, who canceled the Red Line rail system that would have connected West Baltimore to the rest of the city and region—two months after the Freddie Gray protests, and after the project had already secured $900 million in federal funds.[3]

And they didn't talk about the state officials who proposed cutting $36 million from the city's school budget[4] during the same year the Freddie Gray protests were happening—but approved $30 million to build a youth jail in Baltimore.[5]

When I returned to Baltimore, I ran into family members and friends who wanted to move to Atlanta, which has a thriving Black middle class that's featured in television shows and magazines. What they didn't know was how Atlanta had been able to expand its city limits when Baltimore couldn't. Atlanta was able to annex affluent areas like Buckhead in the 1950s and '60s to expand its tax base and compensate for white flight.[6] But Baltimore couldn't because Maryland voters approved an amendment to the state constitution in 1948 that made it virtually impossible for the city to annex any part of the wealthier surrounding counties to add to its depleted tax base.[7]

When I returned home to cover the protests, I felt like I had returned to South Central. The people in my hometown were as hopeless and cut off from the rest of the world as that young Black man in Los Angeles who told me he wanted to make a baby before he died.

My racial pessimism deepened as the years passed. It eventually infiltrated a place that I saw as a sanctuary: my church in Atlanta, Oakhurst Presbyterian Church. After Donald Trump was elected president in November 2016, I attended a neighborhood meeting at Oakhurst. Nibs called the meeting to ask people how the church could respond to the new political mood in the country and invited community leaders to speak. An anxious crowd gathered in a meeting hall in the church. Some people were on the verge of tears, while others clenched their jaws in anger. Some people cited Scripture, while others said that the hope generated by Obama's election was a mirage.

One exchange stood out. It took place between a community leader and an Oakhurst member. The community leader was a white native of South Africa who still spoke with a distinct Afri-kaner accent. He was a middle-aged man who looked like a former surfer: ponytail, tanned leathery skin, and a tattoo of a dragon on his left ankle. He said he knew how scary it was to wake up in a country you no longer recognized. He told people to be practical. The people who had voted for another vision of America weren't going anywhere. "You have to reach out and understand them," he told the crowd, some of whom looked as if they wanted to punch him in the face. "Not everybody who voted for Trump is a racist."

A momentary quiet settled over the room as people looked at one another, some rolling their eyes. The meeting hall was deco-rated with emblems of racial reconciliation. Photos of white, Black, and brown Oakhurst members having picnics, taking communion, and going on mission trips to Central America adorned the walls. Pamphlets about racial justice and flyers alert-ing people to upcoming protests were neatly arranged on a table, near a coffeepot and a tray of glazed donuts.

The white community leaders who sat next to the South Afri-can nodded in agreement after he spoke.

A Black leader at Oakhurst, an attorney with genteel southern manners whose hair always seemed perfectly coiffed, stood up, her eyes blazing. "Why is it that we always have to understand white people?" she said, her voice trembling with anger.

The Black members in the audience stirred in their seats.

"That's right!" someone shouted from the back of the room.

She looked down at the white people sitting next to her and scanned the room before returning her attention to the commu-nity leader sitting at a table at the front of the room. "Why is it that we always have to reach out to them, no matter what they do to us?"

More shouts of agreement spread through the room. She sat down, still looking at the man, whose face had turned red. He said nothing in response.

I wanted to stand up and say amen. I'd felt that anger long before the 2016 presidential election. Meeting my white family didn't liberate me. It added a burden I didn't want to carry anymore. I, too, was no longer interested in reaching out. It was exhausting. I wanted to go out of the trying-to-understand-white-people business. I just wanted to be left alone to live my life.

But someone had other plans.

I don't remember exactly when it happened. It could have been weeks or even months after the Oakhurst meeting. But I do remember what I felt in the moment and what followed.

I stirred awake one morning, rubbing my eyes, and saw that Terry was already sitting up in bed. She was looking at me, eyes wide like saucers. I patted my T-shirt. It was soaking wet. So were the bedsheets.

My mind was too fuzzy at first to be alarmed by my soaked shirt.

"Why wouldn't you wake up last night?" she asked me.

"What do you mean?"

"I tried to wake you up last night, but you wouldn't. I kept saying, 'John, wake up! Wake up!'" she said as the pitch of her voice grew higher.

I sat up in bed.

"Your grandfather was here again last night," Terry said.

I felt the same cold shiver wash over my body, the same goosebumps on my forearms.

"No," I told Terry. I hopped out of bed and looked at her. Maybe this was a joke.

The grim expression on her face said otherwise.

I returned to bed and placed my arm around her shoulder.

"Tell me what happened," I said.

It was the same pattern as before: She awakened suddenly; she saw the same elderly white man in a suit, standing above me by the side of the bed. He was peering down at me with a furrowed brow as if he were trying to decipher a riddle.

She then looked down at me and shook my shoulder, frantically trying to wake me. But she said I wouldn't even stir. "It was as if you were dead," she said.

She cried.

I hugged her tight.

"You left me all alone again, staring at that man," she said, her head buried in my still-wet T-shirt.

My mind was spinning. *What is going on?* I thought. *Why is this happening to me? What does he want?*

I felt a new emotion now: anger. A man had come into my house and terrified my wife, and I had done nothing to stop it. I felt violated.

"Let's have breakfast and talk about it later," I said.

I hugged her and then led her downstairs to our kitchen.

After we ate, I asked her to tell me the story again, looking for some clue that would give me a glimmer of what course of action I could take. I kept asking her to repeat the story until she balked.

"I told you everything I know," she said.

"I just don't get it," I said. "He didn't want anything to do with me when he was alive. Why now?"

Over the next couple of days, I couldn't stop thinking about the visit. I was a notoriously light sleeper. How could I not wake up when my grandfather entered the room and Terry shook me? Perhaps it was a self-defense mechanism, a way to shield myself from a traumatic experience.

I had to do something. I needed advice. It had to be from someone special. I thought of Nibs, but this was outside his box. Nibs didn't believe in demons or ghosts; he saw them as metaphors for racism, greed, and sexism.

I flipped through my mental Rolodex and stopped when I got to one name. He was the most devout Christian I knew, someone with a range of experience and empathy that I had sensed as soon as I met him.

"What about your father?" I said to Terry one morning. "What if I called him?"

I didn't wait for her to answer. I walked upstairs to the bedroom, pulled my phone from the nightstand, and hit a speed-dial button. Terry followed. A man with a rumbling baritone voice and a Spanish accent answered.

"Hello, Alberto? This is John," I said.

I called Juan Alberto Pons, Terry's father, because I respected him so much. He had been married to Terry's mother for more than thirty years and was founding pastor of a church in Erie, Pennsylvania. It was his work as a missionary in Guatemala during the country's civil war that stood out to me.

Terry had grown up in the middle of a brutal civil war that left at least two hundred thousand people dead during a thirty-six-year period. She spent the first nine years of her life living in a military dictatorship. Thousands of ordinary people were kidnapped, tortured, and killed by government soldiers and guerrillas vying for control of the country. She was once kidnapped by government officials and released only after her parents paid a ransom.

Being a pastor in Guatemala was a dangerous occupation. Government soldiers and guerrillas targeted ministers. It was easy to get caught in the cross fire. Her father had once traveled to the jungle to take food and medicine to a Mayan village. The next day, the entire village was wiped out by government soldiers firing from helicopters. If he had stayed an extra day, he would have lost his life. He continued traveling to the villages even after that incident.

He was the father I always wished I'd had.

"Alberto, I wanted to get your advice on something," I said after we exchanged pleasantries. "What I'm about to tell you is going to sound bizarre. . . ."

Alberto said nothing while I recounted the story of the visitation, along with details about my grandfather's racism.

"What do you think it means?" I asked Alberto. "What should I do?"

There was a long silence. Alberto cleared his throat before speaking. He told me that I was the only one who really knew what my grandfather wanted. Then he asked an odd question. "Have you ever been to your grandfather's gravesite?"

"No. Why?"

Alberto said he didn't know what the visit meant; only I would know that. If I went to his gravesite and prayed for his soul, maybe the visits would stop, he said.

"You have to let him know that you forgive him."

I thanked Alberto and hung up. I breathed a sigh of relief. He had taken me seriously—and given me a possible solution.

There was a problem, though. I didn't know where my grandfather's gravesite was. But waiting for the next trip to Baltimore wasn't an option. I had to deal with this now.

I turned to Terry.

"What if we pray now for him?" I said. "It can't hurt."

"Why do that?" she asked.

"Well, I'm a Christian. We're supposed to believe in forgiveness, right?"

I rose from my bed and stood next to the spot where Terry had seen my grandfather. I knelt and held out my hands to my wife.

"Let's pray," I said.

She knelt at the side of the bed and reached for my hands.

I don't remember much of what I said. I told my grandfather that I forgave him, that I was looking out for my mom. I told him that Pat and I had a tough time at first but that many people had helped us.

"I want you to be in peace," I said.

I ended the prayer.

I opened my eyes and looked at Terry. Nothing felt different. I didn't hear any celestial harp chords or angels singing.

I got up and hugged Terry.

She said nothing.

We left the bedroom to get on with our day.

Prayer, though, was just a start. How could I forgive my grandfather if I didn't know him?

And how could I get to know someone who was no longer alive? I had to do what I'd vowed not to do at the church meeting following Trump's election: I had to try to understand a white man who'd hurt me.

There was only one person who could help me do that: Aunt Mary.

I wrote to her, detailing my grandfather's visit. I explained the history. Her father had also appeared to Pat and now Terry. Did she know why? Had she ever had a similar experience?

Her letter arrived about two weeks later. This time I didn't set it aside or wait to open it. I practically ripped it open.

Her response surprised me. "I'm afraid that I can't resolve your questions concerning Granddaddy's visits from beyond the grave," she said. "He was a man of few words and really didn't discuss emotional aspects of his life with me."

That's it? I thought. *That's all you have to say? Your father harasses me, my wife, and my brother from beyond the grave, and that's all I get?*

I didn't give up. Aunt Mary was the only living link I had to my grandfather, besides my mother. She could tell me what my grandfather was like. Did he really hate Black people? Did he ever talk about his grandsons? What did he think of my mom?

Now I was the one sending her letters. I supplemented the letters with phone calls. Her responses came in a steady stream of letters in her meticulous handwriting. The man I knew only as a racist came into focus, like the image of a person slowly materializing on a roll of film in a darkroom.

His name was William "Bill" Dailey, and he was born in 1896 in South Amboy, New Jersey. He was, at various times, a mechanic, a machinist, and a janitor. He was a slight man—five foot seven, 140 pounds—who took pride in his appearance. There was a reason he was so formally attired when Terry saw him by our bed. Aunt Mary said he dressed that way when he was alive: suits, starched white shirts, and black shoes shined so often that a person could see their reflection in them. His idea of informal wear was to take off his suit coat inside on a hot day.

He never seemed to have much luck or family stability. He was forced to drop out of elementary school to support his family, which included a brother and two sisters. Child labor was legal in the first half of the twentieth century. He never talked about his family with his daughters, Aunt Mary told me.

I saw him as a villain, but Aunt Mary said he was a devout Roman Catholic who spent his days reading religious tracts. He constantly told his daughters, "Never compromise your principles."

His faith couldn't prevent the loss of his wife. I knew that my grandmother had had a mental illness, but I didn't know how he had reacted to it.

I asked Aunt Mary in a letter how he had reacted to his wife's illness. Did he ever try to explain to his daughters what was happening?

"He would say, 'She's sick,'" she responded. "He never expounded on anything."

I wanted to know more about how he had reacted to my mother getting ill when she became a teenager. Did he know it was mental illness?

"He said your mother had temper tantrums, but I knew it was something worse than that," Aunt Mary said during a phone call.

The more I learned about my grandfather, the more desperate and tragic his life seemed. I knew that his daughters had been taken from him because of his drinking, but I didn't know how hard he had tried to hold on to them and to his faith. He took the bus to see them every Sunday, wherever they were, often taking candy for the other kids.

"Despite all of his faults, he still prayed every day and attended church regularly," Aunt Mary said.

Aunt Mary mailed mementos from my grandfather's life: a picture of my mom's first communion that he had carried in his wallet; his marriage license; one of his religious pamphlets. As I held his objects in my hand, I felt as if my relationship with him had come full circle. He had taken my birthday cards when I was a kid. Now I was holding his personal mementos.

"Mental illness was taboo when I was growing up," Aunt Mary said. "You didn't talk about that type of situation in your family with other people. There was no one to talk to. So he didn't discuss it with friends or peers."

My grandfather died alone in a rented apartment in 1971, three weeks before his seventieth birthday—seven years after I was born. The last person he called before he died was his best friend, "Brownie," a maintenance man, someone who drove to Mass with him and drank one beer with him after Mass ended. Brownie was a Black man.

Aunt Mary didn't know the precise cause of his death. "I think he just gave up on life," she told me.

For the first time, I knew my grandfather's story. At that point, he stopped being a monster to me. He became a person. He became my grandfather. I thought of a quote from a book called *The Alchemist,* a spiritual fable about a shepherd boy. In the foreword, author Paulo Coelho wrote,

> Even if my neighbor doesn't understand my religion or
> understand my politics, he can understand my story. If
> he can understand my story, then he's never too far from
> me. It is always within my power to build a bridge.
> There is always a chance for reconciliation, a chance
> that one day he and I will sit around a table together
> and put an end to our history of clashes. And on this
> day, he will tell me his story and I will tell him mine.[8]

Aunt Mary helped build that bridge of understanding for me.

But I needed more information. I was still puzzled by some aspects of my grandfather's first visit: the footprints in my childhood bedroom and the birthday cards he took from my dresser. I recalled what I felt as a kid after that visit. *Someday,* I sensed, *I'm going to figure this out.*

I finally heard about someone who might be able to help me. His name was Scott, and he was a hospice worker in Chapel Hill, North Carolina, and an author. I contacted him after I read an essay he had written for *The Washington Post* about a common experience he saw in his job. Hospice patients nearing the end of their lives often reported seeing apparitions of long-dead relatives entering their hospital room to assure them that they would be there for them on the next step of their journey.

Here is a guy who knows something about apparitions, I thought when I called him.

We talked several times before I told him about my grandfather's repeated visits. What did those visits mean? I asked.

He told me the same thing that Alberto had said: "Only you know that."

But he still thought he could help. Scott took some days to digest the story. He emailed me some of his initial thoughts and called me several days later.

Scott's take? He told me that my grandfather wasn't just seeking forgiveness. He was sending another message.

Scott first mentioned the footsteps.

"What was that all about?" I asked him.

"He wanted you to know he was there," Scott said. "He left you a trail to follow."

"And the birthday cards?"

Scott said my grandfather was trying to get to know me. Sorting through birthday cards is something a loving grandparent would do to keep track of a grandchild. He said my grandfather didn't want to be known as the man who called my father the N-word and rejected his grandsons because they were half-Black.

"The stories you heard of him were not ones of love and support," Scott said, his voice rising in passion as he pieced it together. "Here's this beautiful child he refused to know. He wasted a precious lifetime. He could have been a sacred memory, but he became a memory of what not to do."

Scott had worked with dying patients for years. He said what made death so hard for some to accept is the same emotion that probably drove my grandfather to seek me out from beyond the grave: guilt over not being there for family.

"The worst feeling in the world is 'What could have been?'" Scott said. "He wanted you to know: *I was here.*"

For the first time I thought, *My grandfather didn't haunt me. I haunted him. Pat and I weren't the only victims of his racism. He was a victim of it too.*

I continued to pray for my grandfather after his last visit. I still do.

Neither Terry, Pat, nor I ever heard from him again.

It was around this time that I also finally built a bridge to Aunt Mary.

That connection wasn't sparked by some otherworldly encounter. It was inspired by a trip to the paint section of Lowe's.

On a spring weekend, I drove to Lowe's near downtown Atlanta to buy stain for my deck. Once inside, I walked to the counter in the paint section to ask for help. Two men stood behind the counter: a shaggy-haired white man who was on the phone with a customer, and a young Black man with a military haircut who stood there alone, with no customers to attend to.

I looked at both men and ignored the Black man. I waited for about ten minutes until the white man got off the phone, and then I asked him for the best paintbrush and deck stain. He mixed a can of stain for me, and I took it home. When I pried open the can and poured the stain into a pan, I could immediately see that something was wrong.

"Damn," I said, loud enough for Terry to open the back door to see what was wrong.

Not only had the Lowe's salesman given me the wrong color, but he also hadn't mixed it properly. The stain was a rainbow-colored mess. Indignant, I drove back to the store and told the white salesman that he had given me bad stain. He denied it. The Black man whom I had ignored happened to be nearby. He stepped in and gave me another can of stain. It turns out he was the manager.

When I took the new deck stain home, I poured it into the pan. Voila. It was the right color.

That's when it hit me. I dropped my paintbrush into the pan and thought about it: *I didn't get the right color because I couldn't see past color.* I had assumed the white man was more competent than the Black man.

Damn, I thought. *I just racially profiled a Black man—and I'm Black.*

I got up from my deck and started walking around in my stain-spotted jeans and kneepads, thinking about the absurdity of the situation. I had written about racism for more than twenty-five years. I had read all the requisite books about racial bias and anti-racism. I had even interviewed giants in the field, like Dr. Ibram X. Kendi, author of *How to Be an Anti-Racist,* and Robin DiAngelo, author of *White Fragility.*

It didn't matter. I had assumed that the white guy was more competent than the Black guy at Lowe's. I made that decision in a millisecond before I was conscious of what I was doing.

I leaned against the peeling deck and thought, *If I can do this with my background, what about others? What about white people?*

And then I thought of someone else: *What about Aunt Mary?*

It was late afternoon. I took off my paint gear, threw it into my garage, and padded to my home office upstairs. And I did something I had never done before. I pulled the plastic crate of Aunt Mary's letters out from under my desk and started reading them— not for references to my grandfather but to hear her story.

When I put the last letter back into its envelope, I leaned back in my creaky office chair and stared out the window. It was dark; the sun had already set.

I looked up at all the books on racism and racial bias I had on my bookshelves. I could come to only one conclusion after I digested what I'd read: *I'm such a damn fool.*

Everything I'd wanted from Aunt Mary was already in her letters.

My crate was full of heartfelt letters where she apologized to me and Pat for her absence from our lives and talked bluntly about her struggles to understand her past and to understand racism.

In one letter, she talked about my grandfather's treatment of my father. She wrote, "Because your granddad seemed to treat his Black friend with respect, I felt he was protecting his daughter (your mom). I never knew how harsh your granddad was with your dad until you told me. I was wrong. What I didn't realize until you pointed out the episode with your dad was that he was prejudiced. . . . I was wrong."

In another, she said she grew up in an all-white world where she hardly ever saw Black people. The teachers didn't even mention slavery, Jim Crow segregation, or the Civil Rights Movement at the Catholic schools she attended.

She said she didn't meet her first Black person until she was twelve or form any kind of relationship with a Black person until she was nineteen, when she befriended a Black co-worker at a local telephone company where they both worked.

"I never thought I was a racist until you defined it," she wrote in another letter, alluding to a conversation we'd had after I sent her a copy of *White Fragility*. "I thought people who kept slaves were the only racists."

She talked about shame: "You avoided filling out Caucasian as your mother's race on school forms," she wrote, citing another conversation we'd had when I talked about growing up ashamed of my mother's race. "I was unwilling to admit that my nephews had a Black father."

She talked about fear: "My heart dictated I contact you, but fear ruled. Fear of alienating my friends. Fear that my family had nothing to offer you."

And she talked about the anger she saw in me: "If you feel you need to deal with your emotions concerning your mom or lack of support from your mom's family, please pen them in a letter to me. No matter how good or bad, you will find I have very broad shoulders. Believe me when I say I will understand any bitterness, loneliness, emptiness, or hatred you may have had or still experience."

Her letters weren't just about making amends. She said she wanted to know me as a person—what books I liked to read, my upbringing, and my relationship with Pat.

For the first time, I thought of what Aunt Mary had gone through, not what I wanted. She had lost everyone to either illness or drinking—her mother, her older sister, and her father. Even during those brief periods when she and my mother stayed with their father, my mother got most of his attention because of her illness. Aunt Mary grew up in foster homes and orphanages; she, too, was a victim of what had happened in my mother's family.

But it was her faith that stood out the most in all our exchanges. I could connect to her because we spoke the same language of faith. She was a devout Roman Catholic. Her letters were full of grace: constantly stressing the need for forgiveness, integrity, and fearlessly confronting one's sins—all leavened with references to Scripture and reminders that she kept me in her prayers.

She told me that she reached out to us at first because she thought it would help our mom. There was another reason: "I will state that God, you, and Pat gave me a second chance."

Now I had a second chance with her. I don't know how long it was after my trip to Lowe's, but several days later I did something I hadn't done in years. I picked up the phone and dialed her number.

"Hi, Aunt Mary," I said when she came on the line. "This is John. Yes, John your nephew. I just wanted to see how you're doing. . . ."

As the years progressed, our relationship deepened. We talked about family matters, about my mother and grandfather. We talked about our mutual faith. And we talked about race. The topics ranged from Trump to Black Lives Matter. I pressed her on some issues; she parried. We didn't agree at times, but we kept talking and writing letters to each other.

And then somewhere along the way, she changed. She texted me columns that dealt with race from writers such as Leonard Pitts, Jr. She called to let me know that she was watching the funeral for John Lewis, the iconic civil rights man, and said, "Wasn't he a great man?" She asked me to send her more books on race.

One day, while talking about a newspaper column she'd read on slavery, she said, "I believe the past can shape the future, whether it be history or reckoning with your own personal flaws. I'm a prime example of that."

She did more than talk, though. She backed her words with deeds.

When she reached her seventies, she started sending me mementos from her life: prayer books, rings, childhood photos. She asked for my permission to make me the beneficiary in her will, quickly adding that if I didn't want to accept, she would understand. She asked me to handle her burial details if she passed before me and if her husband wasn't around.

While talking about burial arrangements one day, she casually mentioned that she had once arranged to be buried next to her father. But she discovered by looking at the cemetery deed that my grandfather had chosen to be buried in a cemetery that once didn't accept Blacks. "That just didn't set right with me," she said. She changed the location to another cemetery, where her final resting place would be next to my mom's.

What was the catalyst for this change? Nothing dramatic. It was contact. It was the same dynamic at work when my father spent those years on ships with white merchant mariners and when Nibs interacted with Black people in Harlem. It was a relationship, steadily built over time through trial and error.

My conversations and letters with Aunt Mary bore fruit in another unexpected way. Not only did I see her and my grandfather in a new light, but she also gave me what was perhaps the most important gift of all.

She helped me discover the mother I never knew.

CHAPTER 9

Rainbows
Day After Day

John (right) with his father and mother

M y mother stands in the middle of a winding country
lane, staring at the camera. A row of tall oak trees in full
summer leaf rise behind her. Her brow is furrowed and
her eyes flash with annoyance. She's not the thin, brittle woman I
knew. In this photo, her frame is wide and sturdy, easily filling out
a shimmering pink blouse she's wearing. She looks as if she's
about to kick a little ass.

This is one of my favorite photographs given to me by Aunt

Mary. I don't know when it was taken, only that Mom looks different. She looks to be in her fifties at the time.

I never liked looking at photos of myself with my mom. In many, she looks at the camera with a vacant stare, and I am glum, barely smiling. But in the photo of my mom standing near the oak trees, she looks alert and vital—her eyes blazing with some of the same life I saw in the photograph my father showed me years earlier.

I'd always defined my mother by her illness.

Aunt Mary helped me see who she was before schizophrenia took over.

I knew a mother who moved robotically because of her illness. Aunt Mary knew the girl who was a graceful swimmer, an athlete who loved softball and roller skates, and a daredevil who would ride her bike at full throttle downhill.

I knew a fragile woman who asked for Saint Jude medals and prayer and had trouble conversing with anyone. She described a sister who was once "chatty, a jokester, and driven to help anyone in need."

I saw a woman who needed protecting. She described a big sister who protected her when they were kids.

Aunt Mary told me a story that brought back unpleasant memories for me because it sounded all too similar to my own experiences. She said there was a cruel woman who ran a foster home where my mother and Aunt Mary stayed. She confined my mom and Aunt Mary to her basement, dressing them up and allowing them to come upstairs only to meet the social worker who came by for regular visits. When my mother was about thirteen, the foster parent trotted her and Aunt Mary out before the social worker in the living room like always. "She [my mom] told the social worker that she wasn't happy because we had to sleep in the basement or the attic, and that she [the foster mom] was only in it for the money," Aunt Mary wrote in another letter.

Pat started to get glimpses of the same person I was learning more about. He took Mom to a hair salon one day for an appointment. They were early and were waiting in the car outside the salon. Through the window they noticed the hairdresser berating a customer and throwing hair products at her.

"She's a bitch," Mom said casually to Pat as she watched the hairdresser yell.

Pat turned to Mom, suppressing a smile. "Mom, do you know you just said a bad word?"

"I'm sorry, Pat. But she is a bitch."

Hearing about that exchange reminded me of the stories my father used to tell of their dates. The harassment they endured didn't just bother Mom; it angered her. When people would stare at my parents, she would stare right back or say something like "What are you staring at?" or "You act like you ain't never seen people before."

Was her willingness to defy convention and accept people somehow a by-product of her mental illness? But Aunt Mary told me my mom had exhibited an openness and acceptance toward Black people and others before mental illness set in. "She was like that when she was very little, before she got ill," Aunt Mary said. "I never heard your mom say any unkind word about any group of people."

I had focused so much on what my mother had lost to illness that I couldn't appreciate how much of her feistiness, exuberance, and humor remained.

Just as I found a way to connect with Aunt Mary through letters, I found a new way to communicate with my mom: through music and song. Mental illness may have robbed her of some abilities, but not of her love for music. I sent her Tony Bennett and Nat King Cole records and framed posters of musicals she liked. We talked music, and I listened to her merrily sing away.

During one sunny summer visit to Baltimore, I went all in on this approach. Terry, Pat, and I drove to the new group home where Mom was staying in West Baltimore, no more than ten minutes from Aunt Fannie's foster home. We walked toward a handsome three-story home that had a deck on the side. The house was situated on a semi-secluded street lined with trees and retirees sitting on their porches.

When I rang the doorbell, I could hear her voice in the background: "Oh my Lord! Oh my Lord!"

A caretaker opened the door, with my mom peering over her shoulder. When the caretaker stepped aside, I gave Mom a bear hug. She had on a lavender silk blouse and stylish pink glasses setting off her cute pixie haircut. Pat and Terry gave her a hug; then we walked out onto the deck and sat in the deck chairs.

Terry liked to paint my mother's fingernails. But this time I motioned for her to give me some room so that I could scoot my chair closer to Mom. Pat sat in a chair on the other side of the table, looking at me curiously.

"Okay, Mom," I said as Terry handed me the nail polish. "You're about to see me do something I've never done before—put on nail polish."

"Oh my Lord!"

As I held my mother's thin freckled hands, I had a silly impulse. I looked at her and said, "Okay, Mom. Let's sing."

My mother immediately launched into one of her favorite songs, "Que Sera, Sera (Whatever Will Be, Will Be)," gleefully out of tune.

I joined in on the chorus, followed by Terry and Pat.

I applauded Mom after we finished. She smiled while I resumed painting her nails. After one look at my paint job, though, Terry took over.

We talked and joked a little more as the sun started to set. It was finally time to go. I stood up and hugged Mom, Terry capturing our goodbye in a video.

Several days later, after Terry and I returned to Atlanta, I was still feeling the glow from our day with my mom. We were sitting at the kitchen table when I decided to ask Terry a question, one I was afraid to hear the answer to. I took a deep breath, then said, "Do I treat my mom any differently now?"

By this time Terry had spent years visiting my mom with me. She loved my mom like Aunt Sylvia had loved me—through attention to detail. She knew my mom's favorite chocolate, when she was upset, when I was asking too many questions, and what kind of jewelry she liked to wear. She even knew her shoe size, which I could never seem to remember.

She put down her iPhone on the table and gave me a cool look of appraisal. "You used to hug your mom like she was an eggshell and get frustrated when you couldn't talk to her the way you wanted," she said. "And you used to fill up the conversation with a lot of words when you talked to her and started looking at the clock, figuring out when you could go."

"Damn. Was I that bad?"

Terry nodded.

"And now?" I asked.

"You hug her tighter now, and you're not afraid of the silence when you talk to her."

My shoulders loosened in relief.

"How about the photos?" I asked her. "Do I look sad in most of the pictures with my mom?"

"Most of the pictures—until now," she said.

"Why the change?"

"You started to *see* her," Terry said.

A year later, I returned to Baltimore to see someone else who I connected to through songs: my father. By 2018, he was ninety-two. His health regime was as unorthodox as it had been when I was a kid—drinking heavily, smoking weed, and chasing women. He was still going strong enough to inform me one night that only a year or so earlier, he had been with a woman less than half his age. (I didn't ask how that was arranged.) "She couldn't believe that I didn't need any Viagra," he proudly informed me.

That summer, accompanied by Terry and Pat, I visited Baltimore to see my parents. As we gathered one night in my father's living room, Dad reminisced about his days dodging German U-boats when he was in the merchant marine. The conversation somehow turned to his fondness for marijuana, which Pat brought up. My father's jovial mood disappeared, but I didn't know why.

The following day, Pat called to tell me that Dad really wanted to talk to me before I flew home to Atlanta. On my way to the airport, I double-parked in front of his house and walked up to the front porch, where he was sitting in a glider, arms folded and a sour expression on his face.

"Pat said you wanted to talk to me about something," I said as I sat in a chair next to him.

He told me that I should have never talked about his marijuana use in front of my wife.

I sat back in the chair, stunned and hurt. It was Pat who had brought up the subject. But I kept my mouth shut.

"You embarrassed me. You made me feel ashamed," he said, arms still folded.

"I'm sorry, Dad," I said. "I'm sorry." I felt like I was suddenly ten again.

He said nothing and stared straight ahead. I had to get to the airport, so I stood up, kissed him on the head, and said goodbye. He remained silent. As I pulled away in the rental car, I looked back at my father. He was now leaning on the porch railing, a cigarette in his hand. He cracked a small smile and gave me a half wave as I drove off with Terry and Pat.

The conversation bothered me on the flight home. With him being his age, I didn't want any bad feelings to come between us. When I returned home, I wrote him a long heartfelt letter and mailed it. I waited for a reply. And waited. I finally called him two weeks later. After some chitchat, I cleared my throat.

"Hey, Dad, did you get a letter from me?"

"Ah yeah, I got the letter," he said.

"Did you read it?"

"Yeah, I read it."

Silence. I waited for him to say something more.

"Okay, what did you think?" I said.

More silence.

"It was a well-written letter."

"Okay," I said, deflated.

Then he changed the subject.

"I was going to ask you if I could borrow one hundred dollars until next month. I'm expecting some money. . . ."

The next month, just before Thanksgiving, I got a call from Pat. Our father had collapsed that morning and had been rushed to the VA Medical Center in downtown Baltimore. The doctor gave us his diagnosis later that day. Dad was suffering from Stage 4 lung cancer.

Before I made flight arrangements to Baltimore, I called my father's hospital room. A relative handed him the phone.

The once-booming voice had softened, and his speech was so slurred that I had trouble understanding him. His tone was casual, like I'd caught him watching TV.

"Dad! What's going on?" I said.

"Oh, same ol' same ol'," he said.

"Dad, I'm coming up Monday. I can't wait to see you. Patrick will be with me."

"Oh, okay."

"I love you, Dad," I said.

"Okay, I'll see you then, John."

My father slipped into unconsciousness not long after our conversation. When Pat and I arrived at the hospital Monday night, he was barely hanging on. We gathered around his bed and held his hands. The broad shoulders that I'd loved to jump on as a kid were now as shrunken as a little boy's. His arms, once so muscular, were thin, the skin draped over them like wrinkled socks. His hands were swollen, with an IV attached to them, and a tube had been inserted into his mouth. His eyes were closed. The only sounds we heard were the beeping and hissing from the ventilator and monitor.

Pat and I held his hands and were about to pray for him. His left eyelid seemed to move. Pat, noticing it, called out, "Dad! Dad!" his voice taking on an aching, pleading tone I hadn't heard since he was a boy.

Our father didn't stir.

We closed our eyes and prayed. After finishing, we took one

last look at our father. Pat rubbed his left hand. I kissed him on his forehead. And then we walked out into the now-empty corridor.

After our visit, we drove to our father's house and entered his bedroom. Pat wanted to look through his insurance records. I wanted a keepsake from my father, something I could take home with me. I was looking for something else as well.

His bedroom looked as chaotic as I'd remembered. His favorite brown flannel shirt was thrown across his unmade bed. A pair of crutches stood in his closet, and a black-and-white photo of a young Elizabeth Taylor hung on the wall above his small desk. I opened his dresser to search for what I was looking for. I saw a Jehovah's Witness *Watchtower* pamphlet sitting next to a girlie magazine. There was also a black leather Seafarers International Union membership booklet—the merchant marine union where he had experienced the slogan stenciled on the booklet: "The Brotherhood of the Sea." And a weathered moss-green leather pamphlet titled *Basic Handbook on Mental Illness* rested under a pile of papers. I opened a yellow manila folder, and a copy of a newspaper article I'd written when I was in college fell out.

Still, I couldn't find what I was looking for.

Then I heard Pat. "Isn't this great?" he said.

I turned around, and he handed me an envelope with familiar writing on the front. He'd found it wedged against the bed's headboard, between the mattress and the pillow. The envelope had been neatly sliced open at the top. My father had apparently kept it on his nightstand and had been recently reading it.

It was the letter I'd written him only two months earlier, the one he hadn't bothered to tell me he'd received.

I opened it and read some of what I'd written: "Dear Dad, when I was a kid, it was so hard to see you pack and get ready to go to the ship. I knew it meant I might not be able to see you for months. You probably remember how I used to get so sad and beg for you to stay longer.

"As I drove away from your house in Baltimore this past week, I felt like our roles had been reversed. Now I'm so sad that I have to leave you and go back to Atlanta. We had such a brief visit and I wanted to stay longer and talk."

I talked about my mother and Aunt Mary. I told him I no longer wondered about the other side of my family, because Aunt Mary had "filled in the blanks." I told him I admired him for "never developing a hatred of white people despite what you had experienced" and for teaching us to treat people as individuals. I thanked him for teaching Pat and me the words to a Nat King Cole song and singing along with us.

"Anyway, Dad, it was great to see you. Call me anytime. Talk to you later. Love, your son John."

Smiling, I took the letter and slipped it into my coat pocket. I then reached into the closet and took a baseball cap and flannel shirt that belonged to my father. When I brought the shirt up to my nose and inhaled, I could still smell his Old Spice mixed with tobacco.

I was at peace with my father by now. I had spent the last several years taping interviews with him about his life. It had brought us closer and brought me some closure.

What I didn't know, though, was how my mother was going to handle his death.

Pat called Mom to tell her the news.

"Am I going to be able to come to the service?" she said. "I want to say goodbye to Clifton."

"Yes, Mom," he said. "We'll take you."

Pat and I walked into the funeral chapel sanctuary that Friday morning holding our mother's arms carefully. She wore a baby-blue windbreaker, a navy-blue dress, knit gloves, and a gray knit cap. The chapel was filled with family members and well-wishers. My mother was the only white person in the room. As we steered her to a pew in the front, our two older brothers, Twiggy and Tony, stood and gave my mom smiles of recognition. I'd forgotten that they knew her before Pat and I were born.

The pastor delivered a rousing old-style Baptist eulogy that captured the essence of my father's contrarian personality. When he said my father "always walked with dignity," Mom turned to me and said, "Yes, he did."

After the service, Pat and I helped Mom up front to the casket. She looked at our father's body, and her lower lip trembled. She turned to Patrick. "Can I touch him?" she asked.

"Yes," Pat said quietly. "He's at peace now."

My father was buried with military honors. An honor guard draped the U.S. flag over his coffin and snapped to attention to salute him. After the service was over, I stopped by Twiggy's car rental business to talk about Dad. We swapped stories as Twiggy rocked back in his office chair. He told me that Dad had been visiting my mom in Crownsville and group homes for years but hadn't told anyone.

He'd never lost contact with my mother. Even when I was a kid and she was being transferred from one mental institution to another, my father tracked her down. "He always found her," Twiggy said. "And she was waiting for him. That's all that matters in the end."

After I returned to Atlanta, I received a beautifully engraved sympathy card from Aunt Mary. We had invited her to the funeral, but she couldn't make it because her husband was ill.

"Your mom was always so happy and seemed at peace after

your daddy's visits," she wrote. "I often wondered if the visits were motivated by love or obligation, but no matter the reason, your mom was happy. I'm convinced now that he loved her."

After my father's death, Pat and I were responsible for even more of our mother's care. We knew that our father's visits had provided her great comfort. And Aunt Mary visited her almost every week without telling anyone.

But the woman who took care of my mom was becoming too ill to look after her. Pat and I had to find her a new group home. It was an emotionally wrenching experience. People with schizophrenia often need full-time medical care. Mom needed professional care, constant monitoring from people who knew how to administer drugs and provide physical therapy.

We spent several months trying to find a new home for our mom while navigating the byzantine network of social service agencies, hospitals, and social workers to secure funding and medication for her. Pat stepped up like a champion. He took multiple trips to Baltimore to visit her doctors and get power of attorney to control her affairs. (I couldn't do it because her name wasn't on my birth certificate.)

It was during this time that I discovered how my feelings about my mother had deepened.

I was talking on the phone to a social worker from Baltimore's Department of Social Services, trying to find a safe place for my mom to live. I pressed the woman for help, but she was distracted. I started raising my voice, not knowing what else to do. I felt as if I were failing my mom. I had no more arguments to deploy, so I started to beg. "Please help my mom," I said to the distracted social worker.

I thought of my father no longer being able to visit my mom, her time in Crownsville, and all the years she had lived alone, and I blurted out, "My mom is the unluckiest person I know."

And then I burst out crying. I dropped the phone to my side. It was the first time I had ever cried about my mom. It took forty years.

There was silence on the other end of the line. The woman then spoke, her voice softened now. "Let me see what I can do," she said.

We finally found our mom a good and safe group home in West Baltimore. Aunt Mary helped navigate the transition. She stepped up her visits to my mom. We—Terry, Pat, Aunt Mary, and I—became a team. We took turns visiting Mom, and we sent her gifts and clothes and kept tabs on her doctors and caretakers.

Two years after my father's death, Terry and I flew to Baltimore to see my mom and Aunt Mary. I was feeling nostalgic, so I stopped by the home in West Baltimore where I grew up. That nostalgia wore off fast. The neighborhood was as depressing as ever: abandoned homes, shuttered factories, and locked gates keeping people out of the baseball field where I once flew my kite.

I drove from there to Aunt Mary's. It stood near Roland Park, an affluent community in suburban Baltimore. As I drove, the liquor stores, dilapidated buildings, and grimy corner stores disappeared in my rearview window. The narrow streets filled with potholes turned into wide boulevards flanked by trees, lush parks, and handsome single-family homes. I passed a private elementary school and high school that had gated entrances and manicured lawns.

I pulled into a narrow street filled with tidy brick townhomes and saw Aunt Mary waiting for us on the front steps of one.

We hugged, then moved to the backyard, where we sat on

folding chairs to talk about the future. Aunt Mary handed me some documents that contained her own funeral and burial arrangements. She had also selected a final resting spot for my mom. She wanted to be sure I knew what to do if she or my mother preceded me in death.

Then the conversation turned to the past. She talked about how awkward our first meeting had been. She had watched the expression on my face as I drove up in my brother's car.

"You had this dour look on your face, as if you were going to keep a grudge for not contacting you," she said.

"Well, I was mad for a long time," I said, looking at Terry. "I was never that good at disguising my feelings."

We talked about my grandfather, and I thanked her for all the stories, letters, and pictures she provided over the years.

"You helped me a lot," I said to her. "If it wasn't for you, I wouldn't have known about this entire side of my family. You didn't have to do that."

My voice broke yet again. I felt an unexpected surge of more tears but choked it off.

Aunt Mary looked at me intently, silent. "I've learned a lot from you," she finally said. "I can see now how some of the things I did in the past might be considered racist."

Might be? I thought. Years ago, that would have been my cue for an extended lecture on racism and denial. But I no longer felt that compulsion to extract guilt from her. Maybe we would never agree about the past. But it didn't mean I couldn't be grateful for what we had in the present. Now I knew that what was in her was also in me. After all, I'm the race writer who profiled a Black guy in Lowe's.

I stood up to go. The sun was setting, and the streetlights had flickered on.

"Let's take some pictures," Terry said.

We posed. I hugged Aunt Mary. She then hugged Terry, whispering, "I'm so glad you're here."

We walked to the car and got in. As I pulled away, I looked over and saw Aunt Mary standing on the sidewalk, smiling. I waved goodbye.

As I drove away, though, my mood became more sober. I looked to my left and saw floodlights illuminating the gated entrance to one of the most prestigious schools in Baltimore, Gilman School, a predominantly white private school where tuition runs to $34,000 per year for high school students and 100 percent of the seniors go to college.[1] Gilman was one of those white schools that made regular appearances on the *It's Academic* quiz show that I was too intimidated to participate in while in high school.

A quick look at my map also made me pensive. Roland Park was described as the first planned suburb in North America when it was built in the late nineteenth century. It's a predominantly white community filled with Queen Anne and Tudor homes where the median home price is $650,000 and residents live near Johns Hopkins University, an opera house, a symphony hall, and the Baltimore Museum of Art.

It was also built specifically to exclude Black and Jewish people.[2] My father could have never lived in Roland Park when he was a young man. It was built for whites only, becoming one of the nation's first communities to bar Black and Jewish people through racially restrictive housing deeds.

There are people who say that if white and non-white people just learn to love one another like my mother's family and I have, racism will eventually disappear. They see racism primarily as a problem of the heart. It's about people being mean to those with a different skin color.

But that's not enough. A hug wouldn't have allowed my paternal grandmother to buy a home in Roland Park and build up intergenerational wealth for our family. It was against the law. A hug wouldn't have allowed me to attend Gilman when I was a kid. I had to attend an underfunded, racially segregated public school no more than twenty minutes away. Only four people in my entire high school graduating class even attended a four-year college.

The civil rights activist Stokely Carmichael reportedly once said, "If a white man wants to lynch me, that's his problem. If he's got the power to lynch me, that's my problem. Racism is not a question of attitude; it's a question of power."[3]

Carmichael's quote may be apocryphal, but it has stayed with me. So what is enough?

That's a question I've struggled to answer for years. I tried to find the answers in books. I've interviewed some of the most brilliant thinkers about race. And I've covered most of the biggest stories about race in America during the past thirty years.

But none of that intellectual knowledge was instrumental in helping me reconcile with the white members of my family. The relationships I formed with them did more to change me than any book I read, article I wrote, or diversity workshop I attended.

My family's reconciliation has given me a glimpse of what could be enough. It means embracing an old term with a new twist. It's the only way forward for our country that makes any sense to me.

. . .

I've spoken about race before many groups over the years, and I've discovered that if you want to feel the energy leave the room, mention your belief in one word: *integration*. The only word that is more discredited than *integration* is *post-racial*. Both terms are connected to passages in our nation's history when many Americans felt like we were on the verge of transcending our racial divisions.

While there has been some progress, our neighborhoods, schools, and communities of worship remain largely segregated.[4] People were shocked several years ago when a widely publicized poll revealed that three-quarters of white Americans said that they don't have any non-white friends.[5] If that result seems outdated, ask yourself this question: When was the last time you had a person of another race in your house for a social visit?

As a journalist, when I look beyond the numbers that show the persistence of segregation, there's something even deeper that disturbs me. So many Americans no longer believe we can build a genuine multiracial and multireligious democracy. They see diversity as a weakness, not a strength. "Out of many, chaos"—not "Out of many, one"—could be the unofficial motto reflecting our national mood today. I recall an interview I conducted with Yascha Mounk about his book *The Great Experiment: Why Diverse Democracies Fall Apart and How They Can Endure*.[6] He said there is a new generation of Americans who feel either that human beings are too tribal to successfully build a democracy or that racism "is an omnipresent social force of which all whites are inescapably guilty."[7]

"In their minds, 'whites' and 'people of color' will always face each other as implacable enemies," Mounk wrote, referring to some critics of the United States.[8]

Mounk inspired me by detailing why he remains optimistic

about the country's future. But there are others who helped me believe there could be a way forward. I was writing a story about residential segregation when I came across Michelle Adams, a scholar and author who talked in an academic paper about the need for what she called "radical integration." It's a kind of integration that changes attitudes and addresses the need for power. Adams described it as emphasizing not only the value of white and non-white people working and living together but also the sharing of political and economic power.[9]

She quoted author and professor john powell, who wrote, "While desegregation assimilates minorities into the mainstream, integration transforms the mainstream."[10]

Adams called this kind of integration "radical" because it's a sharp break from how integration has traditionally been practiced and because it goes to the root of the problem: the persistence of white and non-white people living in separate worlds. She said, "Radical integration is not a milquetoast acceptance of cultural assimilation, instead it demands: (i) true social, economic, and political enfranchisement for all blacks . . ."[11]

She quoted powell again: "It does not assume that blacks will benefit if they sit next to whites and some of their whiteness rubs off on them."[12]

Radical integration isn't some secret formula that will erase all our racial problems if people follow the directions. There are other names for what Adams described. Some scholars and activists prefer using terms such as *socio-economic integration* or *genuine integration*. Mounk talked about creating "a thriving diverse democracy" where members of different ethnic and religious groups are treated equally.[13] The Rev. Martin Luther King Jr. championed this form of integration in his epic "I Have a Dream" speech, when he painted a picture of a future America where "the sons of former slaves and the sons of former slave owners will be able to sit down together at the table of brotherhood."[14]

People differ on the policy choices to build this new America. But all are making essentially the same point: There is no way we can save our democracy without committing to a vigorous form of racial integration that's different from what we've practiced before. Separate but equal—the legal doctrine that was used to justify Jim Crow in the nineteenth and twentieth centuries—almost destroyed our democracy. An updated version where whites and non-whites live in largely separate worlds won't work in the twenty-first century either.

There's a reason, though, that integration has never gained a foothold in America. There have never been enough white Americans who embraced the concept. Many oppose it because of what Heather McGhee, author of *The Sum of Us: What Racism Costs Everyone and How We Can Prosper Together,* called "the zero-sum paradigm."[15] If it helps non-white people, it hurts white people. That's why this kind of all-encompassing integration—not the kind that places Black or brown bodies in white spaces—"remains the most unsettling, radical idea in modern life," as Calvin Baker wrote in his book *A More Perfect Reunion: Race, Integration, and the Future of America.* "The only balm that will make this wounded society whole is a new understanding of and broader commitment to integration."[16]

What's the alternative if we don't work toward that? We will experience something that a former president feared. Journalist Bill Moyers described why President Lyndon Johnson, someone whom he once served as White House press secretary, championed integration.

"He thought the opposite of integration was not just segregation but disintegration—a nation unraveling," Moyers wrote.[17]

The term *radical integration* was at first just a clever phrase that blended idealism and realism for me. But I gradually realized that I've encountered miniaturized versions of radical integration throughout my life. I just didn't know it at the time.

When I joined Oakhurst, an interracial church where white and non-white parishioners shared power, that was a form of radical integration. Black members weren't forced to assimilate to white worship styles or defer to white leaders.

At sea, when my father built relationships of mutual respect with white sailors in a way that he couldn't on land, that was a form of radical integration. He and many of his white shipmates were mutually transformed by depending on each other for survival.

When my magnificent classmates at Howard became the first in their family to attend well-funded schools with white students, that was radical integration. Integration wasn't just about physical proximity for them. They had access to the same resources as their classmates.

When Aunt Mary and I spent years forging a personal relationship that challenged both of us to see beyond our assumptions, that was radical integration. Nothing helped me understand the cost of racism better than my experiences with her and—yes, I'll go there—my grandfather.

Still, it's been hard for me to be optimistic about the future. Being a journalist doesn't usually inspire optimism. There are some who say a critical mass of white Americans will never embrace integration unless they perceive it to be in their self-interest. One of the most succinct explanations for why integration is in white Americans' self-interest was distilled in a 2021 *Washington*

Post editorial with the headline "The United States can embrace immigration and diversity—or decline." It said that the nation's future prosperity depended on how it treated its non-white citizens and welcomed immigrants:

> The United States could capitalize on the advantages
> that come with being an open, expanding, innovative
> country that is increasingly diverse. Or the nation's lead-
> ers could react to the declining demographic dominance
> of [w]hite Americans by fighting a rearguard action
> against ethnic and cultural change, making the country
> more like Japan or some Eastern European countries:
> aging, stagnating and culturally static.[18]

A choice is unavoidable. I once wrote that America is in the middle of another "irrepressible conflict" where white Americans will eventually be forced to choose between becoming a vibrant, "multireligious, multiracial" democracy or a "hollowed out" de-mocracy where one racial group rules the rest.[19] The status quo will no longer be sustainable.

For years, I sought out political leaders, scholars, and activists to cure me of my pessimism. One of them was Leonard Pitts, Jr., a Pulitzer Prize–winning columnist. He once wrote a column about race that explains why change is so difficult. He said that race is a biological fiction and an "artificial construct" that has been used to divide and exploit people for centuries.[20]

Why, then, does the concept of race endure? "It survives, I think," Pitts wrote, "largely because after all these years we cannot imagine ourselves without it, because we are emotionally invested in the intellectually lazy notion that eye shape, hair texture or melanin content can somehow be correlated to individual destiny, honesty, athleticism, musicality, intelligence and worth."[21]

It was only after reading Pitts's column that I realized one of my biggest sources of inspiration had been sitting in front of me for years.

It was my mother.

My mother could imagine a different type of America. In the mid-1960s, a time when many white people couldn't see the humanity of Black people, she could. Yet she did more than imagine. She was willing to lose the support of her family and her community to see a Black man and give birth to their two sons. Why she did this is ultimately a mystery. Was she driven in part by her illness? Would she have seen my father if she hadn't been ill? Did she as an outsider because of her illness identify with other outsiders like Black people? I don't know, and I never will.

What I do know is that it took courage and that it is because of people like my mother that interracial marriage and biracial children are so widely accepted today.

In 1964, around 90 percent of Americans disapproved of marriage between whites and Blacks. Approval of interracial marriage now stands at 94 percent.[22] The Supreme Court and politicians didn't make that happen. Unsung people like my mother acted first when they broke with family and convention to imagine a different America. I now see interracial couples and biracial children everywhere. Most biracial kids growing up today will never experience the isolation I felt.

This was the same dynamic that made gay marriage possible. Ordinary people acted first. Then the courts and politicians followed. Another source of inspiration for me, author Eric Liu, made this point in a 2020 interview with *Forbes* magazine:

Historically, norms change before policy does. The
Civil Rights Act and the Voting Rights Act became
possible only when a critical mass of Americans shifted
towards a norm of equality. Long before the Supreme
Court ratified marriage equality, a norm took hold: love
is love. Society becomes how you behave. Every act,
civil or uncivil, discourteous or courteous, uncaring or
caring, sets off a contagion.[23]

How, then, could I abandon any hope that America could
change for the better? My very existence is a testimony to the
power of ordinary people to remake America.

And none of that would have happened without my mom.
Maybe Terry was right: I finally started to *see* my mom, not her
illness.

A Sign from Above

When I heard the first reports about the Covid virus in early 2020, I thought of my mom. She was part of one of the most vulnerable groups: elderly people in nursing homes.

She did well during the first year of the pandemic. She got vaccinated when vaccines became available. And though we couldn't visit much because of the pandemic, she didn't appear discouraged. The man who ran the group home where my mom stayed told me that they had tried to institute social distancing by requiring residents to sit six feet apart on the couch while watching TV. But that didn't work with my mom.

"She's so popular that we have trouble keeping the other residents away from her," her caretaker, Avon Green, Sr., explained to me when I called to check in. "We had to find a single chair for her to sit in because that was the only thing to keep the other residents from sitting next to her."

Every call of mine was greeted with her signature "Oh boy! Oh boy!" And of course, she had to end each call with "Can you send me a Saint Jude medal?"

But then in January 2022, she collapsed at her group home. An ambulance rushed her to the hospital, where she was diagnosed with a Covid variant.

About two weeks after she was hospitalized, I got a call at 4:03 in the morning. "Are you John Blake, the son of Shirley Dailey?"

"Yes." I leaped out of bed and started pacing.

My heart was racing. It was the call I had been dreading. Mom's already-frail body had been weakened by the Covid virus. She had suffered a heart attack. The nurse said that the hospital staff had been working on her for about twenty minutes. As she talked, I could hear the beeping of monitors and the hum of machines in the background.

The nurse explained that they had taken all measures possible but there was no heartbeat. "Do you want us to continue?"

I didn't know what to say. I sat on a chair in the bedroom.

"You've taken all the measures possible?" I asked.

"Yes. What would you like us to do?"

I slumped forward in the chair, cupped my hand over the phone, and looked at Terry for guidance. She had worked in hospice and had seen people suffer more than they should have under similar circumstances. She placed her hand on my shoulder and gently said:

"John, if they made every effort, it's time to let her go," she said.

I glanced away, then turned to Terry again.

"Let her go?" I said.

"Let her go," Terry said quietly.

I took a deep breath and returned my attention to the phone.

"Let her go," I said to the nurse.

Right after I spoke, I heard the beeping machines on the other end of the line go silent. I ended the call and walked to the foot of the bed, where Terry was sitting. I sat down next to her without saying anything. She hugged me. We then knelt at the foot of the bed, held hands, and prayed. I don't remember what I said, only that I thanked God for allowing me the chance to know my mother.

A ceremony was held at the cemetery in Baltimore about a week later. Terry and I drove up from Atlanta. Pat, with his son, Pat Jr., drove from Charlotte, North Carolina. We gathered with Aunt Mary under a green tent set up for the graveside service. My mother's urn had been placed on a table, next to a bouquet of white lilies. Terry, a former Methodist pastor, insisted on having a going-home service.

We were racing against the clock. The temperature had fallen to the mid-thirties, and snow flurries settled on our faces. I placed my hands in my pockets and shivered as I sat in a chair. The dreary weather seemed to match the occasion. The sky was a sheet of gray, blanketed by clouds. The cemetery was deserted, the grass the color of straw, dormant from the winter. The trees standing in the background of the cemetery were stripped of anything green.

My mom can't even have good luck on the day of her funeral, I thought as I surveyed the darkening sky.

Terry stood up and walked to the table holding my mother's urn. She lifted a Bible from the table and read a scripture from the gospel of John.

Then she asked me to read the Apostles' Creed and asked Pat to recite Psalm 23. After we finished, she looked at Patrick. "Are there any words you'd like to share?" she asked.

Pat stood. He folded his hands in front of him. "I just—" His voice broke. He gathered himself. "I just want to say I miss my momma. She always talked about herself being a Saint Jude hopeless cause, but she was never a hopeless cause. She was always our mother. She'll be with me forever in spirit. I miss her already."

He sat down. I reached over from my chair to pat his knee. I thought about the first time we visited our mom in Crownsville, and the arc of my relationship with her.

When I was a child, I was ashamed of my mother because she was white. When I was a young man, I was ashamed of her because she had a mental illness. But now sitting next to Pat, I felt something I'd never really felt before—pride. Pride over the fact that I was her son.

For many people, she was the lowest of the low, the type of person they would have crossed the street to avoid. She never owned a car or a house or kept a job for long. When we arrived at her group home following her death, we picked up all her worldly possessions: a Saint Jude prayer book, a Kermit the Frog doll, a T-shirt with my name and Pat's stenciled on it. It all fit into a cardboard box no bigger than a microwave oven.

The day before the funeral, I thought of something Aunt Mary wrote me years earlier: "Please do not ever blame your mom," she said. "She was and is a very fragile and sick person. Also do not pity your mom. I truly believe that your mom is one of the chosen ones. Her reward will be everlasting life with God in heaven."

"John, do you have any words?" Terry asked me, snapping me out of my reverie.

I stood up and rubbed my hands together. The flurries were increasing and the temperature was dropping. "All I can say about my mom is that we don't have a choice about how we come into the world," I said, looking at her urn. "She didn't have a choice about the things that happened to her. But we have a choice about how we respond. And my mom, her humor, her resilience, her feistiness, her joy—that she could laugh, that she could do all those things after all that she experienced—is always going to inspire me. And I'm going to take it with me the rest of my life. I hope the way I live will honor her spirit. I'm glad I got a chance to know her and love her."

After we finished speaking, Pat's son played a recording on his iPhone of another song my mother used to sing: "You'll Never Walk Alone." Sarah, a neighbor and close friend of Aunt Mary, joined us under the tent to talk. Aunt Mary took Pat and his son to a spot in the cemetery to point out Mom's final resting site. Aunt Mary's name was on a niche next to Mom's, which she had purchased years ago—to avoid being buried in a cemetery that had once been segregated.

Sarah smiled as she saw Aunt Mary happily chatting away with Pat and his son. She walked up to Terry and motioned toward Aunt Mary. "She wanted a family all of her life, and now she finally has one," Sarah said.

We had to go. The storm was coming.

I said goodbye to Pat and his son, along with Aunt Mary and her friend. As I walked to the car, I saw something on the horizon that made me think that maybe Aunt Mary was right about my mom. She was one of God's chosen ones.

I pointed it out to Terry. "Do you see it?"

Terry nodded and smiled. "Yes, I know," she said.

I got into my car and shut the door. Terry did the same. I turned the car on and took one last look at what assured me that my mom was just fine.

It was the sun, which had suddenly appeared above the cemetery's frigid landscape, breaking through the clouds.

ACKNOWLEDGMENTS

I would not have been able to complete this book without so many people who gave their support and time.

First and foremost, I want to thank my wife, Terrylynn, who sacrificed so much to give me room to tell my story.

Next comes Patrick, my brother, who put up with my endless questions. Pat was a witness to virtually everything I experienced and was invaluable in recovering memories and setting the record straight.

I owe a huge thanks to my brother Twiggy, who became a second father to me. Another thanks goes to my brother Tony and my cousin Reese, who both gave me a beautiful gift when they shared stories of my mom before mental illness engulfed her.

And when I talk about family, I cannot forget Aunt Mary. Without her graciousness, honesty, and faith, we would not be family. Aunt Mary, you said Mom was one of God's chosen ones. So are you.

Outside my family, there are so many to thank. I am so fortunate to have Roger Freet as my agent. Roger, your sharp editorial eye and relentless good cheer kept me going. I'm so blessed to know you.

And speaking of blessings, I cannot forget Keren Baltzer at Penguin Random House. Keren saw the potential in this nontraditional story on race and faith and taught me so much in the editing process. Her steady demeanor and innate decency kept me going when I grew bone-tired.

In journalism, I have another family that made this book possible. Jan Winburn is the first editor I went to with this idea. Her encouragement and advice were critical. Having Jan as my editor at CNN was one of the best things that ever happened to me. A big shout-out goes to other talented journalists and friends who helped me: Steve Goldberg, Katherine Dellinger, Daniel Burke, Thomas Lake, Brandon Griggs, and Leon Carter, my mentor.

Two brilliant authors lent their time and talent to help me as well: Jemar Tisby and Carol Anderson. Carol, every time I talk to you, I feel like I can do anything. Thanks for taking the time out of your busy life to encourage me.

In the spiritual realm, there is one person who stands above all for me: Reverend Gibson "Nibs" Stroupe. Thanks, Nibs, for restoring my faith.

And finally, I want to thank someone who unfortunately did not stay with us long enough to see this book come to life. Mom, I wanted to surprise you by showing you this book, to see how you reacted after seeing your pictures and to hear you go, "Oh boy! Oh boy!" just one more time. Now I see you, Mom. I finally see you.

NOTES

Prologue: A Painful Return Home

1. John Blake, "'Lord of the Flies' Comes to Baltimore," CNN.com, May 4, 2015, cnn.com/2015/05/02/us/lord-of-the-flies-baltimore/index.html.
2. Cal Thomas, "A Laboratory for Failed Liberal Policies," *World,* May 14, 2015, wng.org/articles/a-laboratory-for-failed-liberal-policies-1617285830.
3. James Clyburn, in Leigh Ann Caldwell and Theodoric Meyer, "Clyburn: 'We Still Refuse to Admit That We Have a Race Problem in This Country,'" *Washington Post,* May 20, 2022, washingtonpost.com/politics/2022/05/20/clyburn-we-still-refuse-admit-that-we-have-race-problem-this-country.
4. Yuval Noah Harari, quoted in Ian Parker, "Yuval Noah Harari's History of Everyone, Ever," *New Yorker,* February 10, 2020, newyorker.com/magazine/2020/02/17/yuval-noah-harari-gives-the-really-big-picture.
5. Michelle Adams, "Radical Integration," *California Law Review* 94, no. 2 (March 2006): 261–311, larc.cardozo.yu.edu/faculty-articles/231.

Chapter 1: Who Can Cling to a Ramblin' Rose?

1. Erin O'Neill, "Sheila Oliver Says 16 States Prohibited Interracial Marriage in 1958," PolitiFact, January 15, 2012, politifact.com/factchecks/2012/jan/15/sheila-oliver/sheila-oliver-says-16-states-prohibited-interracia.
2. "Loving v. Virginia," History.com, January 25, 2021, history.com/topics/civil-rights-movement/loving-v-virginia.
3. Garrett Power, "Apartheid Baltimore Style: The Residential Segregation Ordinances of 1910–1913," *Maryland Law Review* 42, no. 2 (1983): 289–328, digitalcommons.law.umaryland.edu/cgi/viewcontent.cgi?article=2498&context=mlr.

Chapter 2: Black Boy, White Boy

1. John Blake, "Baltimore Faces Its 'Original Sin' a Year After Riots," CNN.com, April 25, 2016, cnn.com/2016/04/22/us/baltimore-future/index.html.
2. Alison Knezevich, "Baltimore Population Drops Below 600,000, the Lowest Total in a Century, Census Estimates Show," *Baltimore Sun,*

March 26, 2020, baltimoresun.com/maryland/baltimore-city/bs-md-ci
-population-estimates-20200326-nebck2k2anbwrcfsbknphsfgwi-story.html.

3. Eduardo Porter, *American Poison: How Racial Hostility Destroyed Our Promise* (New York: Vintage Books, 2021), 135–36.

4. Barbara Basler, "Black Man Is Killed by Mob in Brooklyn: Attack Called
Racial," *New York Times,* June 23, 1982, nytimes.com/1982/06/23/
nyregion/black-man-is-killed-by-mob-in-brooklyn-attack-called-racial
.html.

Chapter 3: Can I Get a Witness?

1. Donald Trump, quoted in Peter Baker, "Trump Assails Elijah Cummings,
Calling His Congressional District a Rat-Infested 'Mess,'" *New York
Times,* July 27, 2019, nytimes.com/2019/07/27/us/politics/trump-elijah
-cummings.html. See also John Blake, "There's a Sobering Truth to
Trump's Racist Tweets That We Don't Like to Admit," CNN.com,
July 15, 2019, cnn.com/2019/07/15/us/trump-tweets-two-americas
-blake/index.html.

2. Carroll Bogert and LynNell Hancock, "Analysis: How the Media Created
a 'Superpredator' Myth That Harmed a Generation of Black Youth,"
NBC News, November 20, 2020, nbcnews.com/news;us-news/analysis
-how-media-crated-superpredator-myth-harmed-generation-black-youth
-n1248101.

3. Michael Winerip, "Revisiting the 'Crack Babies' Epidemic That Was
Not," *New York Times,* May 20, 2013, nytimes.com/2013/05/20/
booming/revisiting-the-crack-babies-epidemic-that-was-not.html.

4. W. Joseph Campbell, "Skirting the Media's Role in the 'Crack Baby'
Scare," Media Myth Alert, April 18, 2010, mediamythalert.com/
2010/04/18/skirting-the-medias-role-in-the-crack-baby-scare.

Chapter 4: The Patron Saint of Hopeless Causes

1. Tom Marquardt, "Tragic Chapter of Crownsville State Hospital's Legacy,"
Capital Gazette, June 5, 2013, capitalgazette.com/cg-tragic-chapter-of
-crownsville-state-hospitals-legacy-20140730-story.html.

2. Kalani Gordon, "From the Archives: Crownsville State Hospital," *Baltimore Sun,* January 15, 2015, darkroom.baltimoresun.com/2015/01/
crownsville-state-hospital/#1.

3. Pamela Wood, "Film to Document Crownsville Hospital's History," *Baltimore Sun,* October 24, 2013, baltimoresun.com/maryland/anne-arundel/
annapolis/bs-md-ar-crownsville-film-20131024-story.html.

4. DeNeen L. Brown, "Emmett Till's Mother Opened His Casket and Sparked the Civil Rights Movement," *Washington Post,* July 12, 2018, washingtonpost.com/news/retropolis/wp/2018/07/12/emmett-tills -mother-opened-his-casket-and-sparked-the-civil-rights-movement.
5. Simon Goddard, "How Petula Clark and Harry Belafonte Fought Racism Arm in Arm," *Guardian,* April 2, 2018, theguardian.com/music/2018/ apr/02/how-petula-clark-and-harry-belafonte-fought-racism-arm-in-arm.
6. Ira N. Brophy, "The Luxury of Anti-Negro Prejudice," *Public Opinion Quarterly* 9, no. 4 (Winter 1945): 456–66, academic.oup.com/poq/article -abstract/9/4/456/1823682.
7. Rutger Bregman, "Science Shows the Remedy for Hatred and Prejudice Is as Simple as It Is Revolutionary: Contact with Our Enemies," *Correspondent,* August 31, 2020, thecorrespondent.com/668/science -shows-the-remedy-for-hatred-and-prejudice-is-as-simple-as-it-is -revolutionary-contact-with-our-enemies/76454927328-119e225b.
8. William Geroux, "The Merchant Marine Were the Unsung Heroes of World War II," *Smithsonian,* May 27, 2016, smithsonianmag.com/history/ merchant-marine-were-unsung-heroes-world-war-ii-180959253. See also "U.S. Merchant Marine Casualties During World War II," USMM.org, August 26, 2006, usmm.org/casualty.html.
9. Brophy, "The Luxury of Anti-Negro Prejudice," 466.
10. Bregman, "Science Shows."
11. "Causes—Schizophrenia," NHS, November 11, 2019, nhs.uk/mental -health/conditions/schizophrenia/causes.

Chapter 5: And Love Comes Gushing Down

1. Sarah Carr, "In Southern Towns, 'Segregation Academies' Are Still Going Strong," *Atlantic,* December 13, 2012, theatlantic.com/national/ archive/2012/12/in-southern-towns-segregation-academies-are-still -going-strong/266207.
2. John Blake, "Harris Dropped a Bomb on Biden That's Bigger than Politics," CNN.com, June 30, 2019, cnn.com/2019/06/29/us/harris-biden -black-people-forgiveness-analysis/index.html.
3. Sarah Pruitt, "Brown v. Board of Education: The First Step in the Desegregation of America's Schools," History.com, March 16, 2021, history .com/news/brown-v-board-of-education-the-first-step-in-the -desegregation-of-americas-schools.
4. Nikole Hannah-Jones, "It Was Never About Busing," *New York Times,* July 12, 2019, nytimes.com/2019/07/12/opinion/sunday/it-was-never -about-busing.html.

5. Peter Piazza, "New Research: Benefits for White Students in Integrated Schools," School Diversity Notebook, February 17, 2021, sdnotebook .com/2021/02/17/new-research-benefits-for-white-students-in-integrated -schools.

6. Rucker C. Johnson, in Valerie Strauss, "Why School Integration Works," *Washington Post,* May 16, 2019, washingtonpost.com/education/2019/ 05/16/why-school-integration-works.

7. Russell Contreras, "The Resegregating (and Diversifying) of U.S. Schools," Axios, January 13, 2021, axios.com/2021/01/13/schools -segregation-increasing.

8. Nina Totenberg and Wendy Kaufman, "Supreme Court Quashes School Desegregation," NPR, June 29, 2007, npr.org/2007/06/29/11598422/ supreme-court-quashes-school-desegregation.

9. Niraj Chokshi, "The Most Segregated Schools May Not Be in the States You'd Expect," *Washington Post,* May 15, 2014, washingtonpost.com/ blogs/govbeat/wp/2014/05/15/the-most-segregated-schools-may-not-be -in-the-states-youd-expect-2.

10. Hannah-Jones, "It Was Never About Busing."

11. Hannah-Jones, "It Was Never About Busing."

12. Nikole Hannah-Jones, "How the Systemic Segregation of Schools Is Maintained by 'Individual Choices,'" interview by Terry Gross, NPR, January 16, 2017, npr.org/sections/ed/2017/01/16/509325266/how-the -systemic-segregation-of-schools-is-maintained-by-individual-choices.

13. Matthew 10:39.

14. Galatians 3:28.

15. Martin Luther King, Jr., interview, *Meet the Press,* April 17, 1960, kinginstitute.stanford.edu/king-papers/documents/interview-meet-press.

16. Romans 10:9.

17. Luke 24:32.

Chapter 6: An Unexpected Meeting

1. Galatians 3:28.

2. Darrell Dawsey, "Gang-Related Killings in County, City Set Record in '89," *Los Angeles Times,* January 12, 1990, latimes.com/archives/la-xpm -1990-01-12-me-257-story.html.

3. Justin Fenton, Darcy Costello, and Tim Prudente, "Baltimore Tried New Ways to Stop the Violence in 2021, but Homicides and Shootings Remain Frustratingly High and Consistent," *Baltimore Sun,* January 1, 2022, baltimoresun.com/news/crime/bs-md-ci-cr-year-end-violence-20211231 -nhiw6lykgzbofginwehe57cohq-story.html.

4. Dennis Romero, "The Militarization of Police Started in Los Angeles," *LA Weekly,* August 15, 2014, laweekly.com/the-militarization-of-police-started-in-los-angeles.

5. Daryl Gates, quoted in Ronald J. Ostrow, "Casual Drug Users Should Be Shot, Gates Says," *Los Angeles Times,* September 6, 1990, latimes.com/archives/la-xpm-1990-09-06-mn-983-story.html.

6. Daryl Gates, quoted in "Coast Police Chief Accused of Racism," *New York Times,* May 13, 1982, nytimes.com/1982/05/13/us/coast-police-chief-accused-of-racism.html.

Chapter 7: Momma, Can You Dance?

1. Ephesians 2:14.

2. Kriston Capps, "How Real-Estate Brokers Can Profit from Racial Tipping Points," Bloomberg, March 3, 2015, bloomberg.com/news/articles/2015-03-03/a-new-paper-examines-blockbusting-and-how-real-estate-brokers-can-benefit-from-stoking-racial-fears-in-white-neighborhoods.

3. Tom Gjelten, "Multiracial Congregations May Not Bridge Racial Divide," NPR, July 17, 2020, npr.org/2020/07/17/891600067/multiracial-congregations-may-not-bridge-racial-divide.

4. Christopher John Farley, "The Gospel of Diversity," *Time,* April 24, 1995, content.time.com/time/subscriber/article/0,33009,982839,00.html.

5. Farley, "The Gospel of Diversity."

6. Catherine Meeks and Nibs Stroupe, *Passionate for Justice: Ida B. Wells as Prophet for Our Time* (New York: Church Publishing, 2019), 102.

Chapter 8: Talking to the Dead

1. Ishmael Reed, "Ishmael Reed: 'All the Demons of American Racism Are Rising from the Sewer,'" interview by Sagar Jethani, Mic, May 1, 2013, mic.com/articles/38965/ishmael-reed-all-the-demons-of-american-racism-are-rising-from-the-sewer.

2. Sergeant Major, "CNN's John Blake: 'I Like to Shame Whites,'" Stormfront.org, May 27, 2017, stormfront.org/forum/t1212996-2.

3. Sheryll Cashin, "How Larry Hogan Kept Blacks in Baltimore Segregated and Poor," Politico, July 18, 2020, politico.com/news/magazine/2020/07/18/how-larry-hogan-kept-black-baltimore-segregated-and-poor-367930.

4. Michael Dresser, "House Panel Finds Money for Education, State Employee Pay Raise," *Baltimore Sun,* March 13, 2015, baltimoresun.com/politics/bs-md-budget-decisions-20150313-story.html.

5. Erin Cox, "State Approves $30 Million Youth Jail," *Baltimore Sun,* May 13, 2015, baltimoresun.com/maryland/bs-md-youth-jail-20150513-story.html.

6. Dan Immergluck, "How History Made This Atlanta Neighborhood a Secession Battleground," interview by Noel King, Vox, February 16, 2022, vox.com/2022/2/16/22937599/buckhead-atlanta-today-explained-noel -king.

7. John Blake, "Baltimore Faces Its 'Original Sin' a Year After Riots," CNN .com, April 25, 2016, cnn.com/2016/04/22/us/baltimore-future/index .html.

8. Paulo Coelho, foreword to *The Alchemist,* trans. Alan R. Clarke (New York: HarperOne, 2014).

Chapter 9: Rainbows Day After Day

1. "Affording Gilman," Gilman, gilman.edu/admissions/tuition.

2. Nehal Aggarwal, "Roland Park Bears Legacy of Racial Exclusion," *Johns Hopkins News-Letter,* November 3, 2016, jhunewsletter.com/article/ 2016/11/roland-park-bears-legacy-of-racial-exclusion.

3. Stokely Carmichael (speech, University of California, Berkeley, October 29, 1966), americanradioworks.publicradio.org/features/blackspeech/ scarmichael.html.

4. Kate Blackwood, "Panel: Segregation Still 'in Force' in U.S. Schools, Neighborhoods," Cornell University College of Arts & Sciences, November 23, 2020, as.cornell.edu/news/panel-segregation-still-force-us -schools-neighborhoods.

5. Christopher Ingraham, "Three Quarters of Whites Don't Have Any Non-White Friends," *Washington Post,* August 25, 2014, washingtonpost .com/news/wonk/wp/2014/08/25/three-quarters-of-whites-dont-have -any-non-white-friends.

6. Yascha Mounk, "An Author Who Studies Diverse Democracies Shares What He Sees as the Future of the U.S.," interview by John Blake, CNN .com, May 21, 2022, cnn.com/2022/05/21/politics/diverse-democracies -mounk-blake-cec/index.html.

7. Yascha Mounk, *The Great Experiment: Why Diverse Democracies Fall Apart and How They Can Endure* (New York: Penguin, 2022), 16.

8. Mounk, *The Great Experiment,* 16.

9. Adams, "Radical Integration," 261–311.

10. john a. powell, quoted in Adams, "Radical Integration," 302.

11. Adams, "Radical Integration," 302–303.

12. powell, quoted in Adams, "Radical Integration," 302.

13. Mounk, *The Great Experiment,* 166.

14. Martin Luther King, Jr., "I Have a Dream" (speech, Washington DC, August 28, 1963), American Rhetoric, americanrhetoric.com/speeches/mlkihaveadream.htm.

15. Heather McGhee, *The Sum of Us: What Racism Costs Everyone and How We Can Prosper Together* (New York: One World, 2021), xxi.

16. Calvin Baker, *A More Perfect Reunion: Race, Integration, and the Future of America* (New York: Bold Type Books, 2020), 32, 35.

17. Bill D. Moyers, "What a Real President Was Like," *Washington Post,* November 13, 1988, washingtonpost.com/archive/opinions/1988/11/13/what-a-real-president-was-like/d483c1be-d0da-43b7-bde6-04e10106ff6c.

18. Editorial Board, "The United States Can Embrace Immigration and Diversity—Or Decline," *Washington Post,* August 16, 2021, washingtonpost.com/opinions/2021/08/16/census-results-immigration-diversity.

19. John Blake, "There's a Sobering Truth to Trump's Racist Tweets That We Don't Like to Admit," CNN.com, July 15, 2019, cnn.com/2019/07/15/us/trump-tweets-two-americas-blake/index.html.

20. Leonard Pitts, Jr., "A White Southerner Searches for the Source of His Family's Racism," *Washington Post,* September 2, 2016, washingtonpost.com/opinions/a-white-southerner-searches-for-the-source-of-his-familys-racism/2016/09/01/c5456bc6-5f3f-11e6-af8e-54aa2e849447_story.html.

21. Pitts, "White Southerner Searches."

22. Justin McCarthy, "U.S. Approval of Interracial Marriage at New High of 94%," Gallup, September 10, 2021, news.gallup.com/poll/354638/approval-interracial-marriage-new-high.aspx.

23. Eric Liu, "Sworn Again: Americans Recommit to a Civic Creed," interview by Ashoka, *Forbes,* April 23, 2020, forbes.com/sites/ashoka/2020/04/23/sworn-again-americans-recommit-to-a-civic-creed/?sh=5250bafe618e.

ABOUT THE AUTHOR

JOHN BLAKE is an award-winning CNN journalist. He has been honored by the Associated Press, the Society of Professional Journalists, the American Academy of Religion, the National Association of Black Journalists, and the Religion Communicators Council. A recipient of the GLAAD Media Award, he has spoken at high schools, colleges, and symposiums, and in documentaries on race, religion, and politics. John Blake is a native of Baltimore, Maryland.

johnkblake.com
Twitter: @johnblakecnn